# Keeping Kyrie

A true story of faith, family, and foster care

# Keeping Kyrie

A true story of faith, family, and foster care

Emily Christensen, Ph.D.
with Nathan Christensen

HWC
PRESS

2016

First Printing: 2016

ISBN-10: 0-9977588-1-3
ISBN-13: 978-0-9977588-1-8

HWC Press, LLC
P.O. Box 3792
Bartlesville, OK 74006

housewifeclass@gmail.com
www.housewifeclass.com
@housewifeclass

Ordering Information:

Special discounts are available on quantity purchases by corporations, associations, educators, and others. For details, contact the publisher at the above listed address.

U.S. trade bookstores and wholesalers:
Please contact HWC Press.

*To my Nathan, whom I love,*

*and who has endured mortality with me*

*that we might live eternal lives celestially.*

# ACKNOWLEDGMENTS

With deepest gratitude, I acknowledge the brilliant editing of my husband Nathan, who took the dramatic documentary of our life together and created a masterpiece, painting my own hot tears into art.

I am deeply grateful for my children, their willingness to share our story, and their very good behavior on days Mama got up too early to write.

I am also grateful for my word-loving friends who so patiently edited with fresh eyes and a keen sense of grammar. I especially thank Tricia, Laura, Krysten, Lisa, Jeanne, Janice, Jen, and Steve, for letting me fill their inboxes with revisions and graphics for approval.

My heart is full of love for our survival team that served our children so faithfully: Anqunetta, who met us at the emergency room every single time, even post-adoption; Deb, who always made sure we had anything we needed, plus some; Laura, who did the job of ten people; and Carie, Allison, Liberty, and Beth.

Thank you Rabbi Ruth Alpers and Reverend Marianne L. Brandon Wilson for your songs, prayers, and blessings.

I am grateful for the staff, sponsors, and many volunteers of RMHC, for caring for me as well as Kyrie, for meals, and for the many rides back and forth across the street.

I thank the concierge team at Cincinnati Children's, without which we would not have been able to pull off our unexpected stay in Cincinnati.

I appreciate the advocacy of Patrick H. Conway, MD, at CMS/CCSQ, and his team who helped us navigate Medicaid.

Many thanks to C. Conley Tunnell and Daybreak Family Services for so generously keeping me on staff through so many hardship events, and much gratitude to Jacob George, Ken Blank, and Frank Clawson for my CPE training and the integrating of Emily.

We also offer our sincere thanks to the Evanson family and the ward in Cincinnati, for so graciously hosting us so often, for so kindly caring for the children while we spent hours and hours at the hospital, and for *Doctor Who*.

There are many who helped us keep Kyrie alive and well:

Without Queen Kristie or The Bumpus, we would not have a Kyrie, period, and we are grateful for their good care in keep her safe and healthy.

Without Krysten, Tracie, and Sherry, we would not have a Kyrie who can play and chatter and move at all, and we are grateful for their work against all odds.

Without Dear Doctor Dave, we would not have understood the battle, and without Lisa, we would not have known how to fight.

Without Nathan's parents, Leon and Mariana, and without our church family, we would not have been able to function during so many emergencies and crises.

The love and support of our entire community empowered us to become a family, support our family, and celebrate our family.

*Thank you.*

*The Spirit of God hath made me,*
*and the breath of the Almighty hath given me life.*

Job 33:4

# 1

It's a long drive, the forty-five minutes that turn into eons when you have a baby that can't breathe. She sounded like a vacuum cleaner caught on the cord of the drapes, and her lips were blue and her hands purple. I watched her tiny form, face down in her prescription car seat bed, in the rear view mirror as I drove. The miles stretched before me like one of those dreams where you are running but can't get anywhere. I nearly cried when I could finally see the hospital, and then again as I got frustrated in the maze of access roads and parking lots. My hands tangled in the seat belts, trying to get her out quickly, and I was scared to death we would lose her before we made it inside.

We were rushed back to a small room in a far corner. A tiny bundle on the adult size hospital bed, she was suddenly covered in cords and face masks and stickers all plugging her back into the matrix of life. Nurses peppered me with questions while doctors hovered over the baby. I was grateful when the baby's caseworker burst into the room, confirming my answers and signing paperwork. A tech brought in some formula, and the caseworker and I both shouted at the same time that she would choke without thickener, without special bottles, and without careful pacing.

Just two months old. She'd come to us from the hospital just three weeks before, fighting for air. Now she had new problems: her little heart was trying to quit.

In less than thirty minutes from squealing into the parking lot, they had a plan for us and a Life Flight was on the way. Her birth mother was notified we were at the emergency room and that the baby could die, but she did not come. When the transport team arrived, the caseworker turned to me and whispered, *You're going. This is your baby, and you're going.* Before I could respond, they strapped the baby to my chest, and then strapped me to an ambulance stretcher, along with her oxygen and monitors, and wheeled us out. An ambulance drove us to an airport, where the stretcher was pushed onto an airplane.

The nurses on the flight were kind, and I was grateful. The four-hour ride was smooth, but very uncomfortable. I could not move because the baby and I were immobilized. My legs were straight out in front of me and soon fell asleep with burning tingles and pricks. The baby also slept. She stopped breathing twice, and all kinds of alarms went off. They moved so fast on that tiny plane, and worked on her while she was still strapped to me. I felt helpless, in the way, and in the dark. I could not move and there was nothing I could do.

Trapped there, lifted farther and farther away from Nathan, the children, and our little home, I felt sucked out of my life like a spirit leaving a body.

*This is just like what happened to my mom.*

My mother was killed on the weekend after my brother and I had gone to the temple to honor the first anniversary of our father's death.

It started with a text message, from a woman who said she was an ambulance, which was very confusing. Her next message said that she knew I couldn't hear to talk on the phone. Her third message, which I now realized was coming from my mother's phone, asked me to have Nathan call her immediately.

Nathan was already talking on his own phone in our nursery-without-babies, working with his writing partner to get ready for an upcoming performance of their musical *Broadcast*. The second it took me to leap from my chair in the study and fly into the nursery across the hall felt like hours. I burst into the room, unable to speak in complete sentences, signing frantically. Nathan jumped up, hanging up on his composer, somehow understanding enough to call my mom's phone. I could not hear what the woman-who-was-an-ambulance told him, but I saw his face. I saw his face, and I knew that day was going to be a bad day.

He tried signing to me as he listened, interpreting what the ambulance EMT woman said to him. *Accident. Broken arms. Broken legs. Cardiac arrest. Heart stopped. Intubated.*

The words made me cold, each phrase punching the air out of my body and pouring ice into my veins. I could not stand up, my legs collapsing under me. Nathan grabbed me, slowing down my fall, sinking us to our knees where he wrapped me up in his arms and began to pray. I did not understand why we were on the floor, or how I got there, or why Nathan was slowing me down with a prayer when I couldn't move anyway. That's when the phone rang again.

*You have ten minutes to get here.*

By then, I couldn't even think in complete sentences. They said they would call us back, but we needed to get to the hospital in Pryor, Oklahoma, which was an hour's drive. We flew into action, some part of my body remembering the four months of my dad dying of cancer, so that my arms automatically reached for toothbrushes, snacks, and a change of clothes as I packed a bag to go to the hospital.

My mind was racing, thinking about how difficult and long her recovery would be, how I would work more to pay for it, how I would not leave her side until she was okay. I kept packing things, reaching for something to hold on to, until Nathan grabbed me and held me and somehow gently shouted, *"This is not cancer! We have to go now!"* He was saying something about no time to pack, that this wasn't about her being in recovery for months, that this was about getting to her before she died. I was so confused. I was angry that people were talking about my mom, who wasn't dead, because I just saw her last night.

While we drove, we called my brother, telling him the pieces we knew. Then the phone rang again, redirecting us to a regional hospital in Tulsa. Nothing was making sense. We turned the car around, heading back in the opposite direction. The hail started then, and the drive to Tulsa seemed to take days. Time stood still, stretching out into one gasp for breath, with tears and prayers and impossible waiting. It made me cold, my own not-breathing.

My mother was notorious for sending misspelled text messages full of words other than what she intended.

4

The irony was that her degree was in English, and her professorial command of grammar came to rule our entire lives, in all its ceaseless demand for perfection. But ever since her ovarian cancer and chemo ten years before, she had pampered herself with manicures that gave her long and fancy nails, which meant she could no longer type well on a touchscreen. She chose to just send random four word messages, rather than keeping shorter nails, so that any text we got from her was a game of decoding. It was even more confusing when auto-correct was thrown into the mix, and I think it amused her.

The last text message I got from my mom was around lunch time, and it said "aprons poolside". I finally figured out that meant that April, her favorite poodle, was still inside her house and my mom wanted me to let her out. I went in the afternoon to do that, and to deliver some treats that my mom loved. After I let the dogs out, I set up a pile of cookies and candies, making just enough of a mess to annoy her, but knowing she would be surprised and delighted. I turned around to see what else I could do in her house, and a sudden stillness fell on me like a mantle of cold snow. It was a deep and heavy eeriness. I did not like the feeling, so instead of doing anything more at the house, I went home to Nathan.

Later, Nathan's phone gave a hail warning for the evening, so he went over to her house to bring the dogs back in. Three little poodles went right to their crates ("castles", my mom would say), but April, the spoiled favorite princess, ran straight to mom's room and hid under the bed. Nathan gave up trying to get her out and started to leave, but right as he got to the door, he heard a sound like a sad cry. He turned around, and saw April crawling out of mom's room on her belly. She made it all the way to Nathan, and then rolled over on her back. Not an affectionate animal to anyone but my mom, this was weird. He rubbed her belly, picked her up, and put her to bed. We didn't know that mom's car had just collided with a Jeep and a semi, but somehow, April did.

Mom was very proud that she had gotten a job of her own so that she could move out of my house when Nathan and I got married. She had retired from her library work years ago, but she was a career woman and did not like *not* working. She wanted to be independent in every way, and thought of her new rental house one block over as a kind of wedding present to us. She had worked so hard finding a job, and so many had (illegally) treated her unfairly because of her age. She was so proud of her work, and had been so courageous in facing those challenges.

Her reward for so many years of survival were her grandchildren, whom she loved more than anything, even more than the poodles. She wanted nothing more than to be a grandmother, and wanted any and all of them staying with her as often as possible for as long as she could get away with before my brother and his wife noticed. When they grew into teenagers and got busy, she went to their events and activities, driving for hours just to get to watch them play or perform, and putting on a brave face as if she were content with quick smiles and drive-by hugs. She was so proud of them!

That's what she was doing that day: driving back from Missouri, where she had watched one granddaughter in a swim meet and another win the debate tournament. It was unusual that I was not driving her, but these were daytime events, and she had done a good job of leaving in the afternoon so she would be home before dark. I was enduring morning sickness, and felt strongly that I should not go that day.

Later, when I said so many times that the accident was my fault because I was not driving her that day, Nathan would remind me this was false guilt, even survivor guilt. He said that when the driver of that Jeep hydroplaned and clipped the front of that semi, coming to a stop right in front of mom's car, there was no time for her to even hit the brakes. He said if I had been driving her, I would have died, too. We could be real about how much we missed her, but also consider for what purpose God kept us alive — because we did survive, though I didn't feel very alive without any air.

Nathan was amazing during his first emergency with me. He got the after-hours number for sign language interpreters, and called the hospital on the way, giving them the number and explaining that mom was being flown in, and I was her Deaf daughter with cochlear implants, and that we needed an interpreter to be sure nothing was missed and everything understood.

Nathan held me up those days, and often held me tight. I think he helped me not run away. When information was too hard to face, and scenes too gruesome to see, he kept me steady and strong in a way I have never known. He comforted me when I cried in my sleep. When I jolted awake in panic and screams, he wrapped his arms around me. When I laid there unable to sleep, still and quiet but with tears pouring down my cheeks, he rubbed my hands and just let me be.

He kept working hard at his job as a writer through all the chaos, knowing that I needed time off from my full-time work as a counselor for Daybreak Family Services. Trying to support us alone, he served me while I was in a daze, going with me to the funeral home, and stopping me randomly to look in my eyes and remind me to breathe. He brought me bits of food from the piles carried in by friends, and took me for little walks so there would be air in my lungs.

He gently reminded me there were only two weeks left in the month, and that we must move quickly to get mom's things out of her rental home. He moved all her costume jewelry over to our house so I could give pieces to my nieces, and he helped me go through her clothes. She had so many that it would take me three years to get them sorted, but he never complained or rushed me. He fed her dogs. He did the dishes, swept the floors, and took care of my garden. He held my hand, always quietly in the background or slipping gently forward to make me laugh until I was breathing again. I loved him, and was glad he was the husband I had chosen.


It seemed like hours before we made it to the hospital that Saturday night in the cold sleet. I broke out into hives as we rushed into the ER. Nathan went ahead of me, to find the interpreter and figure out where to go. I had to go to the bathroom. Again. And throw up. Again.

Finally making it to the waiting room, I saw Nathan's face, and I knew. When I looked into his eyes, melted with love and grief, I knew. He took my hands and pulled me close, looked me in the eyes with all the courage a brand new husband of only three months could muster, and told me, "She's gone." That was the second time I fell to my knees, screaming and crying. I pulled at my hair and hid my face and sat where he moved me and cried and could not breathe and could not breathe and could not breathe. The doctor came in then, to make the official announcement, saying she had expired.

I was aghast. I was angry. *Expired? Like milk?* I was so bewildered, and so cold.

We learned that my mother had never been brought to Tulsa. The helicopter couldn't lift off in the weather, and she had never stabilized enough for transport. She had been taken by ambulance to a small rural hospital instead, and we were in the wrong place. We had gotten the wrong information that second time, receiving the call meant for the family of the driver of the Jeep that killed her just five miles from the interstate exit that would have delivered her safely home. This is not where my mother's body was waiting for me to say goodbye; this was where the doctors were treating the man who killed my mom.

The doctor said that if we hurried, and if we beat the medical examiner to the correct hospital, we could still see her before her body was taken away. I went into panic, saying over and over that we had to go. My friend René, who had appeared like magic to help interpret and to help grieve, knew how slick the roads were becoming. She grabbed me, and looked me in the face and said sternly, "Go. But do not hurry."

We left the conference room, with me wondering how to make my legs move, and came out into the hospital lobby. Nathan's parents were there waiting for us, and I cried out to them that she was already gone. I needed them in that moment, but also felt my body heave away from them, these in-laws I had only just met and now were the only parents I had, but not *my* parents. My parents, both of them, were suddenly gone, and I was an orphan, and there was no air in the room.

Nathan drove us those forty miles on that cold and icy night. A million thoughts were flying through my head while I was thinking nothing at all. I was frozen like sleet building up on the windshield wipers, tears streaming down my face. Nathan dropped me off at the emergency room entrance of the Pryor hospital, and then tried to follow me in so quickly that he forgot to put the car in park and had to go chasing after it. I ran in to the front desk to ask where to go, and they said trauma room five. My brother and his family were already there when we arrived, their little girls sleeping in an alcove with the oldest brother watching over them.

I blindly ran through the curtain straight into my brother's arms, flashing back to the day my grandmother had died and he ran to me in a similar way. Something about the fear on his face reminded me of his little four-year-old self, while somehow making me feel ancient. The mantle of big sister fell on me the way stillness fell at mom's house earlier.

We did beat the medical examiner, and I was able to see my mother. She was still guarded by the police who had brought her and we could not touch her body, or embrace her, or move the sheet that covered her body. She was the wrong shape, not all together, not herself at all, except it *was* her, and I needed her. I needed to touch her, and to hold her, and to weep over her. I needed to speak to her, to cry out for her to wake up, to scream at her not to leave me. I needed to make sure she knew I was sorry for everything, that I was grateful for everything, that I really did love her more than anything.

The doctor came in with my interpreter to tell us about her injuries and their severity. He talked about damage to her internal organs, and he told how long her heart had stopped, and that it had stopped so many times they ran out of medicine to get it started again. He said that when the accident happened, her nerves were cut so she was not in pain, and we got to talk to the EMT who stayed with her. She said mom was just chatting away, telling her all about her daughter in Owasso and the day she had spent with her Springfield son and his children at their high school competitions in Joplin.

It was when the firemen cut her out that all the pressure was taken off her body, they explained. She had been pinned down under the crushed dashboard, her legs crumpled in front of her. She was helpless and trapped there, unable to move, and there was nothing she could do. The metal pushing her down had been blocking her injuries, so that her heart had enough pressure to keep beating. But when they removed her from the wreckage, there was nowhere for all the blood to go, and it all just left her. She lost consciousness immediately.

She died then, he said. He said even if they had been able to revive her, she would not have ever been herself again – nothing more than a vegetative state – with her brain missing oxygen for that long, not even taking into account her other injuries.

My interpreter, Don, was good and brave and did his job well. His heart is real, and his spirit authentic, and his eyes were wet as his hands flew. I am glad it was him on call that day. They amaze me, those interpreters and the gift they are to the world. I will never forget his hands from that day, or the shapes they made in the air, those shapes in the air I could not breathe.

When the doctor finished, the policeman told us about the accident. He said all the eye witnesses told the same story, and that mom was not at fault. He said there was nothing she could have done. He told us about the Jeep and the semi, and that she hit them directly right after they came to a halt in her lane. He said anyone in the car with her would have died, too. "I should have been driving her," I said. *I should have been driving.*

They let me have a final moment alone with my mother, then. The information of what had happened to her had been poured into the air around me but wasn't processing in my mind. My brother went to deliver the news to his children. Nathan went to tell his parents and bring them to the room where our family would be gathering.

My mom was all covered with blankets, except for her face. Her belly was swollen three times its normal size, which would not have impressed her, but I knew from my work in the ER that this was where her blood had pooled when it could not be pumped through her body. Her face was the only thing that was mostly okay, and to me she was beautiful. She was not herself, and my mind was fighting to put this picture together, that it was my mom there on that stretcher. I knew it was. It was her hair, and her skin, and her closed eyes. *Wake up, Mama! Wake up! Please.* Even as I whispered these cries, I knew I didn't really want her to wake up, not to what she would be facing. *How can I ask you to wake up only to endure so much?* My little girl heart needed magic right then, magic to make her okay, and magic to make none of this happen, and magic to make me never to have been naughty, so that I would be worthy enough to work some magic.

When there was no magic, and I was suddenly no longer a daughter but a grown woman with no parents, I kissed her forehead and brushed my hand through her hair. I held her hand and I cried in whispered prayer tears. Then the medical examiner showed up and took her away.

We gathered ourselves in an empty room, because gathering is what Mormons do. Our local bishop and his wife came, and Nathan's parents, and my brother's family, and Nathan and me. Nathan, together with the other men, laid hands on our heads and gave us each a blessing. A stillness came, with words of strength and comfort that were specific to each of us. This was the power of the priesthood, the peace from our Heavenly Father, even the understanding that hard things are a part of His plan.

Nathan and I drove home silent and exhausted, his hand holding tightly onto mine. I didn't want him to pull away, but I had nothing left in me to squeeze back. When we got home, it was nearly two in the morning. We were starving, and I spun myself in circles trying to function enough to make some food. Nathan vacuumed, because it was the only chore we hadn't finished before the accident, and I was obsessing about it, knowing my family would be sleeping on the floor. He didn't argue or reason with me; he just did it so I wouldn't have to worry about it.

I found leftover surprise in the freezer, and threw it in the microwave. When it was thawed and I pulled it out to see if it was warm, I realized it was leftovers from the roast we had with my mom at Family Home Evening the week before. That was my first time to cry since leaving the hospital, and my first time to hit one of those endless, random triggers that would continue to pop up like ghosts and throw her absence at me like a knife in the gut.

Around three in the morning, with my brother's family sleeping in every available corner of the house, the organ donation people called for the long interview required for them to do whatever they do. My brother and I bumbled our way through answering their questions about when she had ovarian cancer and who else had cancer and what kind of treatments did she have. We were exhausted enough that we got silly, trying for anything besides more crying. When they asked if mom had ever had rabies, he said, "Yes, and her name was Emily." When they asked when mom's high blood pressure started, I told them it was the year my brother was born. We finished by four in the morning, but before we could sleep, they called back to apologize and tell us there was not enough left of mom for them to be able to harvest anything, and so her body would just go directly to the funeral home for cremation. Nothing was funny after that, not for a long time.

My last visit with my mother had been something special. Nathan and I had gone to the doctor to get our medical clearance for fostering. He examined Nathan and talked to him, and gave him a shot, and then signed his papers. Then he saw me, examined me, and told us he would sign my papers, but that we needed to know that I was pregnant again. When I told mom, she said she already knew. Moms are like that. She talked with me about my high risk for miscarriage, and talked to me for the first time about her struggles to carry a child, and her experiences when she was pregnant with me. It was sacred beyond just being our final conversation.

That's why I wasn't driving her that day, when she had asked for a ride to Joplin. She wanted to go see my nieces compete in their events, but I had morning sickness and couldn't go. She didn't want to miss it because nothing made her happier than a whole day with all the grandchildren. In full role reversal, I made her promise to be back before dark. *Why didn't you come home? You promised, Mama! You promised!*

I lost that baby three weeks after my mother's funeral. I didn't really lose it, but that's how people talk about death, as if the person was misplaced or might turn up later. The idea might be intended to distract or ease the pain, but it wasn't truthful. What was true is that my baby had moved from one world to another, had transformed from a mortal being into someone eternal.

I thought of my mother every time I "lost" one of my babies. I felt like a pioneer girl from children's novels that I had read long ago, left on my own in a new and unfamiliar world with strangers, albeit kind ones. I knew she would have been with me had she still been alive, and wondered if she had now gained some sacred access to my children that I did not have. Perhaps her lifelong promise to come back and haunt me was more than just an idle threat.

# 2

Landing in Cincinnati, we were transferred from Life
Flight to ambulance, and rushed to Children's Hospital.
Nurses and medics whisked our gurney through
hallways and back elevators. We arrived on the
Complex Airway Unit at four in the morning. This
wasn't just any middle-of-the-night hospital admission.
The whole team was there: a doctor, nurses, an Ear Nose
and Throat (ENT) resident, a respiratory therapist, and
a tech who brought me water and diapers, and who had
already made up a bed for me next to the tented crib.

It was incredible, that moment we were swarmed by
people who knew what they were doing, who knew
how to keep my baby alive. The helicopter team
unstrapped me and helped me sit, swinging me to the
side of the gurney so my legs could wake up before I
tried standing. Someone was giving a report, someone
else was checking the baby's vitals while she was still
strapped to me, and nurses wheeled in a scale and new
monitor stickers. No one stole her from me, though, and
they worked together seamlessly as I gently unhooked
the carrier straps from my chest to free her from the
cocoon that brought her here. This was my moment of
birthing her, bringing her from the womb of our first

17

months fighting for her life, and delivering her to the doctors who would help her finally breathe.

The nurse was gentle when I handed the baby over, and something in me broke with relief when I saw the nurse rest her on her belly on the scale. I didn't have to tell them or argue with them or beg them not to weigh her on her back. *They knew.*

Now, in Cincinnati, with breakfast waiting for me, and a warm bottle of formula for the baby in the right kind of cleft palate valve-ed bottle, I cried. Like a girl. Exhausted and far from home, I knew we were in the right place. This baby was going to live. I had never felt so alive with hope.

As soon as I could, I looked for a quiet corner to FaceTime Nathan. If I could just see his face and hear his voice, I would not feel so far away.


My whole history with Nathan seemed to be one of reaching out, whether it was falling in love from a thousand miles away, or searching for that almost-remembered someone for all the years before.

I hadn't been on a date since I got baptized — becoming a full-fledged Mormon had been traumatic enough. It took me nine months to sort out the mess of my life in order to prepare for baptism. I took the year after that to remain single and alone, and it was one of the most healing things of my adult life.

But my new-found faith helped me to see my family for the miracle they are. And it led me (finally) to the idea of repeating the process, to creation, to wanting to take what I have experienced and create my own family. I had to start dating, that's what it came down to, really.

As soon as word got out at church that I was ready to date, grandmothers and sisters and mothers began setting me up with their grandsons and brothers and sons. But somehow I struggled to even get to the point of being Goldilocks, with enough choices to be picky.

There was a double date with good friends, which felt like it would be less pressure. I dressed nicely, and tried to relax and not be too nerdy. I got to the restaurant first, and waited in my car to see him before going inside. I was immediately intimidated. The guy who walked up with our mutual friends was older than me, but I could see how we might be a cozy fit. I got out of the car and waved, and they called me over to join them.

My friend held the door open for his wife. My date cut in front of me, stepping inside and letting go of the door — which closed right in my face. He sat across the table from me instead of next to me, so the couple had to adjust themselves as well. The music in the restaurant was loud enough that my cochlear implants had trouble distinguishing their words from the background noise, and I only caught snippets of his monologues about anime and movies I had never seen. The waitress came and he ordered first, then traded his menu for a phone pulled from his pocket. He played on his phone for the entirety of the meal.

There was no conversation between us, and I grew more and more silent as I slowly gave up trying. Finishing his sushi before the rest of us, he pushed back his chair and stood to comment on how good the meal was before walking out the door. He did not pay for his meal or mine. We did not exchange eye contact as he left without saying goodbye, and it was not with excited anticipation that my cheeks burned.

Another guy told me after dinner I was only a 5 and he was looking for a 10. I just stood there, blinking, and wondering how on earth a coding system had been developed – and why didn't it include a talent or interview portion?

The next morning, I went to the gym (mostly because that is what made me a 5 instead of a 2), and the more I thought about any guy judging me like that, without knowing me at all, the harder I worked out. I hit the racquetball court hard, and then did laps in the pool to erase any evidence of tears, because a jerk like that does not get any tears from me, not even hot-angry-tears, not even one.

I sat in the sauna until my muscles melted. I needed to rest and reclaim the Emily that I knew me to be, have some prayer time, calm down, and take a few deep breaths. Except it was hot in there, so I didn't sit for long, and decided to scratch "sauna" off the coping skill list.

This stayed in my head as I drove to work. I knew that any guy who would even think such rude, shallow, juvenile things is only revealing who he is and his own lack of substance. I knew that any guy who reduces girls to a number was not the kind of guy I was interested in – at all.

The guy that I would marry would be okay with me as I am, in an authentic it-doesn't-matter kind of way, not just a demeaning or oh-it-matters-after-all way. The guy I would find would be one of soul strength, with a capacity to endure, and he would be faithful and kind above all else, and he would never condemn me for my past or weaknesses or mistakes. Because I am not finished yet. I am a work-in-progress. That's different from a guy being a piece-of-work.

I ranted like this at the office, where I worked part-time as a counselor for LDS Family Services, while my coworkers roared with laughter. Mocking me, they came up with a new idea to introduce me to someone completely different than any of the people I had previously dated. The other counselor had a cousin in New York who was also a writer, who created musicals and song lyrics. "He's a lot like you," my coworker said, "and really funny. He served his mission in Korea, and I think he is a temple worker now." He pulled up his Facebook and Twitter accounts, and showed me some short quips that made me snort. Amused but wanting to cut short this inquisition, I tweeted a few snarky responses to some of the cousin's one liners.

The cousin snarked back.

I replied with a long Facebook message, explaining apologetically what had happened and why I had contacted him. He replied almost immediately, and I don't remember the rest of that day. Our messages went back and forth, as if we were sitting on opposite sides of the ocean, dropping notes in a bottle.

He was in New York and I was in Tulsa, the perfect beginning for writers. Everyone around me was in shock that I was dating a boy from New York. They must have had doubts, but they would just ask me, "Are you happy?"

I got to smile in a way I didn't even really understand, and say, "Yes."

We were happy enough that we needed to meet in person. He announced that he would be meeting family in Utah in June, and helping his parents drive back to Oklahoma that weekend. It was like a romantic comedy adaptation of *The Odyssey*, this crazy journey we were on to find each other. I wriggled through office time and paperwork, talked through client crises and transferences, and negotiated my way through cancellations and reschedules. Every moment ticked by in slow motion.

I never got nervous, but when my calendar told me our first real date was that very day, the excitement began to pump through me, no longer restrained. I tried to make sure I looked decent and smelled pretty, workday and all, but then later I took my car for an oil change – and that gave me an odd, mechanical smell. But we were grownups, and fairy tales are harder at thirty-five.

A text message came. He had arrived. He was there at the park, ready for me. A million things raced through my mind, while simultaneously my spirit came to a halt, in a good and sacred way, the way time stops at the temple. There was a complete peace, a depth to something I could almost remember, a stillness of the sort that only happens just before the morning sun breaks the horizon into dawn. *Today is the day*, I thought.

It was a summer solstice I will never forget. I pulled up to the park, very focused on being quite grown-up. Except then I squealed when I saw him, and ran right to him like a crazy girl. He was waiting, watching for me from a long way off. We rushed to each other like a couple of saps, and I very nearly cried my eyes out. It was amazing. Good. Perfect. Whole. Home.

Nathan took my hand immediately, leading me to follow the path around the lake. It was hot, and we laughed at our sweaty hands. Our walk on that first date was a lot like our marriage turned out to be: blissfully happy together as we sidestepped the goose poop of life.

Talking with him was easy, and we were as delighted with each other in person as we had been in our letters and phone calls. We found a bench under the trees, and our stories unfolded: growing up, favorite books, dreams of the future. Our first day together, and already the week ahead felt too short. But he had surprises planned, starting with meeting his parents for dinner.

We drove back to his parents' house, with its charming front flower beds and porch swing. His mother eagerly pushed past the glass door before his father could get it all the way open for her, and I was immediately overwhelmed with hugs. I was embarrassed to learn that his father, after dropping Nathan off at the park, had lingered in the parking lot just in case I turned out to be creepy, and he had heard my squeals of excitement.

The next night, the tables were turned, and Nathan came to meet my mother. His parents joined us at my house for dinner, this being the first time they met my mom. I made gluten-free noodles with a pesto sauce and pine nuts, grilled chicken, steamed broccoli, and toasted sesame bread with hyssop from a recent trip to

Israel. Everyone was so good and kind and thoughtful and delightful, truly, even when all I had to offer for dessert was the last of my Easter candy from two years before (which they finished off quite nicely).

While chatter at the table continued, I slipped away to get ready for our next date adventure: ballroom dancing. For the first time ever, I called mom in to give her approval on my outfit. She gave me a thumbs up, and I gave her a hug. We excitedly whispered about how much we loved Nathan and his family. It's moms like that who keep a girl's head on her shoulders long enough to dream big.

We made our way across town to the elegant ballroom studio where I knew most of the couples by name. The instructors were the husband and wife who first introduced me to the church. I knew Nathan could dance because he told me he had taken classes in college, and anything he didn't know he was eager for me to teach him.

Nathan took my hand, dancing me into an embrace. When my favorite foxtrot began to play, he led me around the floor confidently but gently. When he noticed older ladies sitting alone at their tables dance after dance, he started taking turns inviting them to waltz. When a samba came on, he was comfortable asking for help with the steps.

I knew by the end of the week that Nathan was the man I wanted to marry. He knew it, too, and we drove all the way to Springfield to meet my brother and his family. With my father gone, Nathan felt he ought to ask my brother for permission to marry me, but then ended up chickening out. "It never came up," he insisted. My brother has never let him forget this!

Driving home, I felt prompted to exit at Joplin, and Nathan agreed it would be a good time to stop and eat dinner. Our tire began thumping right as we pulled into the parking lot of a Steak 'N Shake, and completely fell off — shredded — as we rolled to a stop. I don't know what would have happened if we had still been going 75 miles per hour.

Rather than seeing this as an omen of what life together would be like, we laughed, and we worked on it together. I pulled a blanket from the trunk and laid it down so Nathan wouldn't get dirty. He got down on his knees to start wrenching off the lug nuts. I heaved the spare out of the trunk, lowering it next to where Nathan was crouched with the car jack. He pulled off the last lug nut, and I lifted the tire off. While I carried the shredded tire back to the trunk, he put the new tire on and tightened everything into place. He lowered the car as I folded the blanket and packed it away. It was brilliantly done, we thought, and we were very proud of our teamwork — which somehow left me covered in tire mess, while Nathan was perfectly clean.

As I laughed, Nathan unexpectedly dropped down on one knee. I watched his hands move in sign language for the first time. I saw him ask if I would marry him. I laughed again, thinking surely I had misunderstood. I assumed he was offering to buy me a cheeseburger, which is a similar gesture in sign language, and said that was sweet of him. He cleared his throat and said, "No, seriously," before signing his question again. I squealed and hugged him and said yes.

Inside the restaurant, we celebrated with chocolate caramel ice cream as I texted my girlfriends to tell them I was officially engaged. They all wanted pictures of the ring. I didn't have one. Instead, Nathan bought me a little monkey out of the quarter machine, giving it to me as an engagement gift. I laughed, and tried to remain calm.

Driving home, we took the scenic road away from the interstate, through little towns, past mom-and-pop stores, and miles of grazing cattle. There were tall trees along the path, winding curves, and little hills that raised and lowered us like the roller coaster of our unfolding life together. The setting sun was as bright as the light in our eyes. The sky was as open as our hearts. "That's what happens when writers fall in love," Nathan said. There were increasingly ridiculous similes everywhere.

This was our last night together before Nathan went back to New York. Unwilling to go home, he drove us to the park in town where we first met. He reached for my hand as we walked toward the lake. I remember the reflections of the trees, the flickering of the moon in the water, and the fireflies dancing around us. In this perfect moment, he pulled out a small wooden box and opened it to reveal… a necklace. "I couldn't afford a fancy ring," he said, "but I know that you appreciate symbols." From the simple chain hung a metal ring pendant, and fireworks went off in the sky behind us as he hung it around my neck. "I didn't plan that part, but we'll keep it in our story," he said.

Then he said he had another surprise for me, and pulled out the wooden box again. In the bottom, nestled below where the necklace had been, was a real ring. "I couldn't afford this," he repeated, "but this one came from my mother's side of the family." It's not every girl who gets two engagement rings. And an engagement monkey.

I knew in that moment we were creating a new family, and that the end of a lifetime of searching was really a beginning. Our fairytale week was over too soon, and Nathan would be flying back to New York, but the hard months of geographical transition ahead would not be nearly as hard as the first thirty-five years apart. Our spirits were united, finally permitted our reunion in mortality, and there was so much to remember of each other and learn again. It was very good.

We spoke on the phone every night after that, growing our relationship and praying together. We also wrote daily letters, me typing from the summer docks near the lake and him typing on the subway as he rode to and from work. So far away, and yet we were in constant contact.

We made our wedding plans, choosing a simple theme of *words* that fit us as writers. I spent the summer using pages from copies of our favorite books to make all of our flowers, and even came up with paperback bow ties for the men in the wedding party. We would have a typewriter instead of a guest book, and wedding invitations that looked like the beginning of the novel that our life already was and would become.

By the end of summer, we had saved enough for me to fly to New York. I wanted to meet his friends there, and he wanted to share with me that part of his world.

I stayed in the apartment of his bishop's family, and he picked me up every morning for a day of adventures.

There was so much to see and do! We started with a carriage ride through Central Park, which turned out to be less romantic than in the movies, as our third wheel was a very chatty driver. We went to Maker Faire in Queens, and we carried giant lanterns in an after-dark parade in Morningside Heights. One day he took me on a chocolate crawl through Greenwich Village in the rain, and another day he took me for grilled cheese on the Lower East Side, wandering past trendy boutiques and gritty street art. On Sunday, we went to church in Inwood, then rode the Staten Island ferry past the Statue of Liberty, and peeked into the windows of the restaurants of famous chefs.

One night we walked the High Line Park in the Meatpacking District. There were gardens and trees lifted two stories up on a former elevated train trestle, and children flitted about them like lightning bugs. Couples found corners in which to snuggle with snow cones, and roller bladers whizzed past us in the breeze. I could smell the ocean instead of the city, and I felt dizzy with the sensation of being so close to Nathan.

Then there was a beautiful engagement breakfast organized by one of Nathan's friends, held on a perfect summer morning at a park in Fort Washington. I met his friends who were actors and nutritionists, photographers and nurses, musicians and writers, singers and financial gurus. They were all leading lives of intense creation, living the legacy of starving artists, and bonding through the friendship of those who know what it means to breathe in the city.

Our favorite guest, however, wasn't even invited. We were in the middle of introductions when we noticed someone standing a way off from our brunch table. He had a spotted brown face, long white hair with a long white beard past his waist, purple and green robes to the ground, a walking stick, black wire glasses, a tall silver wizard's hat, and a brown dragon puppet on his hand. Nathan went to greet the man, and spoke with him for some time before asking the name of the dragon — at which point the man informed Nathan that he had already been speaking with the dragon. It was a little hard to tell the difference.

The dragon was hungry, so we invited the dragon and his wizard to join our engagement brunch. They gladly did so. We offered some special morsels to the puppet, who declared the wizard to be the keeper of the food. The dragon spoke in a deep voice with a slow drawl that was not quite Scottish, and also occasionally yelled at airplanes passing overhead. The party continued, but we kept an eye on him — part cautious, part curious as to what would happen next.

At last, when he finished eating, he walked slowly over to us in a very stiff and stately manner. He proclaimed, "You have been much more hospitable to me than previous wedding parties I have encountered." He raised his walking stick hand and announced, through the dragon, that because we had offered him breakfast, he would give us a wizard's blessing.

He told us our marriage would be a good one, and that it would last as long as the stars, but that only hard times could make one shine so brightly. He said that we would always be rewarded and blessed for our good deeds and sincere kindnesses, which he knew to be real. He promised our lives would be full of laughter and joy, happiness and festivity, all because – as it turns out – dragons love breakfast. Then, with a swish of his cape, he disappeared, and we never saw him again.

On our last night, Nathan and I sat holding hands by the East River, looking at the stars and the glowing apartment windows of the Bronx, dreaming about our future, and trying hard not to think about being separated once again.

# 3

Living in the hospital meant living the hospital schedule: rounds at six in the morning, shift change at seven, residents and specialists in and out all morning, cleaning crew at lunch time, and then some rest in the afternoons before rounds started again in the evenings. Sleep was limited, and always uncomfortable. I had a small couch that unfolded into a sectional bed, which was a little like sleeping on a flight of stairs. There was a tall cabinet with two drawers, enough for me to hang the few things I brought with me. A window with blinds between the inner and outer panes marked my days and nights, and the small bathroom next to the couch bed gave me light in the evenings when the baby needed to sleep.

She did not get to sleep much. Techs were required to get her full vitals every hour, and the oxygen and heart monitor alarms woke her often. I had to work extra hard to get her swaddled with so many wires and tubes, rock her longer to comfort her with so many extra sounds, and be extra gentle laying her down facing away from the busy unit outside our door. More often than not, as soon as I did, a resident would come swinging the door wide open, pouring light into the room and talking as loudly as if they were on the basketball court with a buddy. The nurses were more careful, so smooth with their whispered entrances, holding the curtain closed against the light as they came in, moving stealthily around the room so as not to disturb her, and sneaking back out again without ever waking her up. Chaplains could do it, too, this ballet of care, dancing into the room for a silent blessing of peace and comfort, and out again without making a sound.

While her rest and healing was most important, there were more reasons it was helpful for her to sleep. Being a thousand miles from home all alone left me some very practical challenges. I needed to find meals, and even if I had them delivered, there was not a single meal I had in eight weeks that wasn't interrupted by someone coming into the room. I also needed a place to do my laundry, which the nurses helped me locate around the corner from our unit. The hospital had a lovely parent center, where I could use the Internet for work or rest away from the hospital room, and there was a chapel where I could go to pray and meditate. When the baby was awake, and doing well enough, and not attached to too many machines, we could walk down to the playroom to continue her developmental therapy exercises from home, and enjoy the normalcy of toys.

I did not get to actually sleep all night until two weeks later, when we finally got into the Ronald McDonald House. That gave me a clean room right next door to the hospital, with my own bed, bathroom, and a desk at which I could write and work. They had meals, a pantry available for me to cook anything I wanted, and mailboxes to receive packages of love from home. They also signed for deliveries as we began getting supplies for feeding tubes and suctioning machines and oxygen. There was a gym in the basement, and I was able to stretch my muscles and walk again for the first time in weeks. They had a full library, a meditation room where I could meet with friends from church to receive the sacrament on Sundays, and a craft room where I made gifts to send to the children back home.

Oh, the children. I loved each one of them so much, but I worried about Nathan home with so many all on his own. For me, though, these weeks of chaos and exhaustion were the first break I had gotten in two years.

Fostering was never an effort to replace having children of our own. It was something consciously and specifically chosen by the two of us in response to spiritual promptings we had received individually, even before we were married. We were in our mid-thirties when we finally found each other, and it made sense in a you-had-to-be-there kind of way for us to spend part of our honeymoon filling out applications to be foster parents. In the short time before the shadow of my mother's death, we filled out mountains of paperwork, got fingerprints taken, had our home invaded for inspections and home studies, completed classes and trainings, and started gathering supplies for children we had never met.

Approval took almost a whole year. It's not supposed to take that long, and it was hard not to worry about children who needed foster homes during that time. Some of our paperwork was lost and had to be done twice, and we were on the waiting list for training classes that seemed to be full month after month. The home study, a lengthy interview process in which both of us were grilled over our family histories, our discipline philosophies, and any other indicator of our parental suitability, took ages to be completed by the contractor and sent back to the state. We waited at least two extra months because our resource worker moved to North Carolina and no one told us.

Jumping through so many hoops helped us understand one more of the many reasons why it is so hard to recruit new foster parents. It's a preparation time, warning foster parents to be ready for how hard fostering can be. The process is daunting, expensive, and exhausting, all before any children arrive on your doorstep in the middle of the night, hungry and scared and naked.

And oh, they did come! There were more than seventy over the next three years. We were a couple of newlywed introverts drowning in other people's progeny.

There were children who came for a weekend, and children who stayed for years. Some got to go home to their families, and a handful left and came back again while their parents worked through new problems. A few children were transferred to therapeutic foster homes for a higher level of care, and still others needed to be hospitalized, unable to cope with the traumas they had endured.

When children enter foster care, their cases are brought before a judge multiple times, though the children themselves are rarely present to witness it. The very first court hearing is a statement of the charges for why the children need to be in the care of the state. The next hearing is to identify any family or friends of family available and willing to foster the child in a kinship placement. If not, and if the child has no one else, then they remain in traditional foster care placements. Adjudication is next, which means the parents respond to the charges against them, and either deny or agree ("stipulate") to the charges. If the parents stipulate, then they receive a treatment plan — essentially, a to-do list of required steps toward getting their children back.

Working a treatment plan could mean anything from domestic violence or parenting classes, to random drug tests, to finding adequate housing and working to pay for it. Any effort at all, any attempt at all, in doing the things required counts as "working" the treatment plan. If the parents do the work, then they get longer and longer supervised visits, then unsupervised visits, then overnights, and then, finally, they get their children back for a trial period before their case closes. If they don't, then their time runs out and rights are terminated. Each court hearing during this process might be little more than a quick check-in on the parents' progress before scheduling the next hearing ninety days later. This was our experience for three years.

Once the Department of Human Services (DHS) decides the parents are not making progress on their treatment plan within the given time frame, the permanency plan for the child is changed to "concurrent adoption". This means it has been decided who will adopt the child if the parents' rights are terminated. It does not mean the child will be adopted, just that a home has been chosen if that becomes necessary. Once DHS recommends termination of parental rights, that doesn't mean the district attorney actually makes a motion for it to happen. Even once they do, there are still more hearings before it actually happens. Even after it does happen, the parents have a right to a jury trial, and that means more months of additional court dates. If they win the jury trial, it doesn't mean they win the child — just more time to work the treatment plan. If they lose the jury trial, an adoption date is set. It turns out that family court is less like Perry Mason, and more like the DMV.

Foster homes can limit the ages they accept, but we took any age. We had detoxing drug babies, fresh from the hospital, that we kept alive and in early intervention therapies until placement with relatives could be found. We had toddlers who thought they were babies, and toddlers who knew how to fend for themselves. We had elementary school children still in diapers, and pre-teens who knew too much about the world and not enough about how to be a part of a family.

One reason so many children came through our home was because we were willing to take sibling groups — brothers and sisters that never quite gelled with us because they were so afraid of letting go of each other. We had twins several times, even one pair that hated us and stole all they could on their way out the door. The most we ever had at one time was nine, for a week when we were overfilled and had a sibling group for short term care as well.

Some experiences were scary, like a teenager's boyfriend driving past taking pictures of our home, or the time a mother on drugs nearly ran us over with her truck. One time we had a five-year-old try to stab her baby sister, and once a teen tried to muffle a baby's cries by filling her crib with blankets. Two separate four-year-old boys tried climbing bookshelves, intending to knock them over onto other children, and one eight-year-old kept punching holes in walls and doors and cabinets and mirrors.

And there was the poop. There was always so much poop! Once we had five children at the same time in diapers or pull-ups, and it was exhausting. Poop in diapers is way better, though, than poop in the shower. Or on the walls. Or hidden in a lunch box in the closet. That was the worst. Mind you, that only happened once; hidden poop is not a normal occurrence in fostering, nor is poop on the walls, though it sometimes happens. Most often, foster children are normal children with normal poop, but with really big traumas.

For three years, we endured screaming, biting, and tantrums from children too old to be kicking and pounding the floor. Beloved treasures around the home were broken, torn, or stained. None of these children were bad children. Many of them had a lot to be angry about, and all of them were grieving. None of them were home with the family they knew.

We had beautiful experiences, too. One family we worked hard with for many months, driving children to visits a county away, facilitating nightly phone calls, and attending court dates. The parents were working hard enough on getting their lives back together that we were able to invite them to join our family for Thanksgiving dinner. It was an incredible thing to witness.

Movement and playtime are so important, especially for trauma healing. When we had some problems with a few of the children being aggressive after visits, we got them signed up for soccer with practice nights on the same nights as visits. It gave them a productive and healthy and appropriate way to get out all that energy without destroying everything around them – or the people around them. It worked great, while also providing a structure for us to each have one on one time with the different children. Because that's what families do. Because that's normal.

One of my favorite lines from our church's official statement, "The Family: A Proclamation to the World," reads: "Successful marriages and families are established and maintained on principles of faith, prayer, repentance, forgiveness, respect, love, compassion, work, and wholesome recreational activities." That must have been echoing in my head when I chose to take five children with me to the ballet. It was really hard. They had never been to the ballet before, and a full-length program is a long time to sit still and be quiet. But I took them because I knew they could do it. I took them because they needed to know someone believed they could. I took them because it was good for their brains, and soothing to their spirits, and a brand new exposure — good for kick-starting dendrites and new neurological connections. I took them because it is art, and beauty, and music, and something good in the world. I took them to experience feeling safe, and nurtured, and spirit fed, and normal for just a small bit of time.

We got better at it over time. We learned how to ask better questions from child protective services, so that new placements were a better fit with the children already here, rather than only reporting how many empty beds were available. We got connected with resources to help provide bedding, clothing, shoes, toys, and equipment, since nearly every child came with almost nothing and left with everything we provided them. Caring for them well meant that each new child who came needed shoes, church shoes, socks, underwear, church clothes, school clothes, play clothes, hygiene items, and school supplies. This could cost up to $1,500 per child without any notice, a true loaves-and-fishes miracle, since there is no way we could have produced that much money again and again and again.

We developed a routine when new children came, making the transition as easy as possible for everyone, including the children already living with us. We would always take a family vote on whether to say yes, so that whatever children were already in our home could have a voice and feel included in welcoming new arrivals. We would order pizza as soon as the new children were on their way, even if it was the middle of the night. When they arrived, Nathan would take whatever they brought with them directly to the laundry room and put everything in the dryer (in case of bed bugs), while I signed papers with the caseworker. The children would eat together while we took them one at a time – me for girls and Nathan for boys – to shower, put on clean clothes from our supply closet, and check hair for lice. Once everyone was cleaned up, we would give the official tour and get conversation started about bedtime.

We always kept things light and easy that first night, because even when we had no idea why the children had landed with us, we knew they had already endured a hard day, and that bedtime would be rough. There were always tears at night. Some of them shared what they had endured, or insisted they didn't know why they were picked up, and some didn't talk about it at all. We never pushed, and it was a delicate balance to be present but respectful of someone else's crying child.

By morning, anything they had brought with them was clean and ready for them to have back, as well as new clothes from our supply closet. This usually translated into early morning excitement, as if it were Christmas, giving us a positive start to the first day. We would then spend the afternoon doing less exciting things like registering them in new schools and taking them for well child checks at the doctor.

Those were very intense times, and it took all the energy from both of us. The worst of it was worthwhile when the child who only screamed started laughing, when the child who had to carry around a peanut butter sandwich left it at home one day, or when families that worked hard on healing were reunited. But the very best of it was that, of all those children who came to our house, there were six who stayed.

The first was Alex, a four-year-old boy with long red curls down to his waist. The TV news reported that he was found wandering in a casino parking lot at four in the morning, wearing only his underwear. He had broken out of the van in which his family had been living, while his parents were inside the casino.

Nathan started Alex's first bath, to get him cleaned up and into pajamas. He was obviously anxious, and the sight of a full bathtub pushed him over the edge. Nathan barely got him wrestled out of his t-shirt before Alex broke into full-body sobs. Unsure how to respond, Nathan pulled the grieving little boy up onto his lap and rocked him as he cried for nearly an hour. Finally scrubbed and into some dinosaur jammies, Alex curled up like a puppy on his bed, where he slept on and off for the next three days.

His first weekend with us coincided with my mother's burial in the tiny farming town of Sparta, Missouri. It had taken our family some time after the funeral to get her ashes returned to us, and then find a weekend when all us could gather together. We wanted to make a good impression on the assembled relatives, so we dressed Alex in a blue shirt with a cream colored suit, and pulled his long red curls back into a ponytail. He got carsick on the winding Ozark roads between home and the family cemetery, and he sat pale and quiet in his booster seat, clutching a Styrofoam cup in case of emergency. By the time we arrived for the graveside service, he was done being still and he spent the time running like a feral child, weaving his way in and out of gravestones.

I was anxious about how my family would respond, but he succeeded in charming them right away. His last name and red hair happened to match a branch of my mother's family, which gave him an in with them. A couple of hours of genealogical research later, it was revealed that Alex and I had, in fact, been swimming in the same corner of the gene pool.

That would be the only pool he'd be in for a while. His fear of the water extended to the one in our backyard. He spent every day that first summer with us in his bathing suit, swim goggles, and arm floaties. He often had a snorkel in his mouth as well. He would sit at the top of our pool ladder watching other children play, but he never actually got in the water. It took a year of pool exposure and swim lessons before he started to splash around and play like the other children.

As he became part of our lives, we learned there were many gaps we had to help fill in, like teaching him how to sleep under a blanket and how to use utensils to eat at the table. When we took him for an eye test, he didn't know what the symbols on the eye chart were, like birthday cakes or horses or gloves. He had not been to church, and spent his first Sunday crawling under the pews and barking like a dog.

He was nearly nonverbal at first. If we asked, "How are you this morning?" he would repeat back, "How are you this morning?" in a chipper robot voice. We started to notice how he would flap his hands and run on his tiptoes when he got excited. The official diagnosis of autism came as he was being assessed to start school. Compounding that, his IQ test results came back with a discouraging score of 52. We held hope that it was more because of lack of stimulation, and lack of exposure to general items referenced on the test, than a permanent condition.

Alex's autism has brought challenges, as well as delightful gifts. Once he started talking, he could quote entire movies and has never forgotten a song lyric. He has since become high-functioning enough that most people probably don't even know that he's different at all, which is a blessing and a challenge, particularly when his behavior is erratic. Three years later, at the end of first grade, his IQ test came back with a score of 98, an improvement which had seemed impossible.

Anber was picked up two weeks later from the same casino that had given us Alex, and brought to us in the middle of the night. She was left in a car seat on the front porch while the caseworker ran back to her car for paperwork, and it was so dreamlike to open the door to find a baby sleeping on the welcome mat.

When Anber first landed on our doorstep, I knew when I saw her face that she was staying. There was something in our spirits that recognized each other, and something that filled me in a way I had never felt before. Something settled in me, and I just knew. It was a profound moment, even if its fulfillment wasn't until two years later, when she was declared officially ours, when she could run and sing and swing and play instead of just sleeping in a carrier with her tiny fingers wrapped around a bottle.

Anber was still asleep from the long ordeal when Alex woke the next morning. I whispered to him that he got a new baby sister in the night, and he jumped out of bed to run and see. He peered over the crib at her sweet sleeping face, then shouted, "Hey, mom! Where'd you get that little brown baby? At the gift shop?" This is still their favorite story, the one in which they met, the one in which they became best friends from the beginning. They have come to rely on each other, two constants in a family in flux.

DHS wasn't sure how old Anber was, but by her teeth they knew she was right around a year. She couldn't walk yet, and her legs were bowed out in the shape of the car seat where she had spent so many hours. She had had so many caregivers, and suffered such neglect, that she already had reactive attachment disorder, a condition leaving her struggling to bond with us and unsure that we were trustworthy. It meant that this sweet baby would stiffen when we tried to hold her. It meant she would rather hold her own bottle and burp herself afterward, than trust anyone else to do it. It meant that she screamed for the first three months, hours on end, venting her rage from a year of unmet needs and unknown traumas.

One day, a caseworker's aide showed up without any notice to take Anber for her first visit with her biological mother. I had to wake her from her nap and get her dressed nicely, which she did not appreciate. The aide didn't even let me put her in the car seat myself, but pulled her screaming from my arms and buckled her in an unfamiliar car seat before driving her away to meet people she didn't remember. It was the worst feeling, to have a baby torn out of my arms, and feel her grabbing for me as she was pulled away. She came home screaming as well, but I didn't know if it was because of the visit or because she was just hungry.

Many of her struggles had to do with food. She screamed anytime she heard anything that might be close to the sound of cellophane wrappers, and initially refused all table food except French fries. When we used the drive through on a road trip, she would scream from the time we placed our order until we could get her food delivered to her hungry little hands. Never confident of when her next meal would be, she would eat and eat, shoveling food in until it was physically painful to take one more bite.

Part of this was because she had rickets, which I didn't know was still possible in this day and age. The pediatrician diagnosed her with this during her first well-child check, when we pointed out her bowed legs and asked about her joints that creaked and clicked like an old woman. Her bones were so soft we could almost feel our fingers press into her bones as we picked her up. She had blood work to confirm it, and we had to give her special vitamins, but mostly she seemed dead-set on eating her way back to health.

One night, we were trying to figure out why Anber wasn't settling down, screaming even later into the night than usual. It turned out that the teenager who shared her room kept giving Anber light-up toys in effort to soothe her, which was actually keeping her awake and making it much worse! Exhausted and frazzled, Nathan told her that *Super Nanny* had said that such toys would keep the child awake for an extra hour, and the teen ran over to Anber's crib and yanked out the toy. Anber finally fell asleep exactly one hour later! That was not the last time I had given thanks for the ability to take off my cochlear implant processors, and turn off my "ears".

Anber also screamed her way through her first family road trip. She screamed at the cabin where we stayed in Branson, Missouri. She was screaming her way around Silver Dollar City, a nearby old-timey Ozark-themed amusement park, when we found a child-sized playground with a slide. She climbed up the steps on her rickety legs, and laughed as she came slipping down the other side. She did this over and over again for an hour! When it was finally time to go and I pulled her away, her reaction was predictable. She was still screaming as we were nearing the exit, when Alex — having an autistic flashback to her first morning —

suddenly shouted, "Mom! Where did you get that little brown baby? At the gift shop?!" It would have been funnier if security had been in on the joke.

Fortunately, Anber was brilliant, the most genius one-year-old I had ever worked with in twenty years as a counselor. She picked up sign language quickly, which greatly reduced the screaming related to getting her own needs met. *Hallelujah!* She could work puzzles, mimic the play of other children, and speak in whole sentences almost from the beginning (though, even now she will barely speak outside the home). In fact, Anber signed for a very long time, other than occasional verbally violent outbursts following visits with her mother that her therapist said were flashbacks. Later, when visits were suspended, she changed almost overnight, speaking verbally at home and even interacting with others besides Nathan and me.

When bringing us placement papers, Anber's caseworker told us she would be short-term because she would be going to family. But later, when her family was ruled out as a placement option, we had to decide whether we wanted to keep her or not, knowing that this might be a possible adoption case. This was after she had screamed at us for three months, and we knew that meant committing to a reactive attachment child long-term. Reactive attachment children *need* that kind of long term commitment, though, and anything else just re-traumatizes them. We prayed about it seriously, and the answer came that it was an honor to have her in our home, whether for a short time or a long time. We told them yes, and so she stayed.

When Alex had first arrived, Nathan was preparing for a theater production. I brought Alex by auditions before even taking him home. He ran around the room, playing with the actors' pens, scribbling on their scripts while pushing his long red curls out of his face. They asked the name of this boy who would come to occupy such a large place in our lives, but we didn't know — he was nearly non-verbal, and being so new, we didn't even have his paperwork yet.

By the time Anber arrived, the show was in production. We had five children by that time, and wanted to take the older ones to see it, but because of her attachment issues we could not just leave Anber with a sitter. Instead, we covertly set up a playpen in the back of the theater. I held her until the show started, then gave her the last bottle of the day to keep her content, and rocked her to sleep in the back row. Then I laid her down, praying she wouldn't wake and add her own shrieking soundtrack to the show.

What initially felt like an onslaught of chaos and exhaustion eventually settled into a routine of adventures. We never knew what Alex would say or do, and Anber taught us a more conscious kind of parenting that was as good for us as it was for the children. When my health deteriorated two years later, we took the summer off from fostering other children. Alex and Anber stayed, and for those two months the four of us had our first taste of becoming family, after so many had come and gone.

# 4

Even when I was weary, this baby kept fighting to live. She gasped and choked and contorted her chin and head, trying to open her own airway enough to get breath. She didn't gain weight because every calorie was used trying to pull air into her lungs, and I didn't know how long both of us could keep trying.

My strength came from saying my prayers as always, even though there was no privacy and the hospital floor was cold and hard. My strength came from my scripture study in the quiet mornings, and with Nathan in our FaceTime evenings. My strength came from priesthood blessings, the sacrament of bread and water, and temple ordinances.

I felt the prayers of those back home like a blanket that kept me warm, heavy with comfort on my shoulders. I knew the things which had been promised, and I believed them. So when they would say she was failing because of this or that, I did not hear their words. I heard only the whispers that told me: *Shift her here. Hold her like this. Reposition her this way. Wake up now! Lift her! Stretch her! Raise her head!* I listened, and I did, and she lived. And I cried. I wept. I wept and her staff wept, because no one could believe she was still with us.

But they could all feel the Spirit, the power of God moving, the breath of priesthood blessings. They felt it even if they didn't recognize it. They felt it even when they didn't know that showing up for work that day and using their skills counted as an act of faith. To me, these staff people were angels of God, and their ministry to me was one of comfort and strength and peace. It felt like a temple there, sometimes, and I knew that feeling was the presence of God.

I relied on that power of God so far from home. If we had been home, Nathan could give the baby a blessing as she struggled to breathe and prepared for surgery. Here, I relied on other worthy priesthood holders to come to us, acting in God's name and by the authority of the priesthood, to lay their hands on her. My prayers could draw down the power of Heaven; their hands delivered the blessing.


I didn't always understand this concept of priesthood authority. I didn't believe that God had delivered power and authority to men on Earth — especially to men. I couldn't have imagined how that would change. The turning point was *Dancing with the Stars*. Marlee Matlin is an icon of the Deaf community, so when she came through Tulsa with the *Dancing with the Stars* tour, I couldn't miss it. I went and watched, and knew that if she could do it, I could do it. I maybe couldn't do it as well as she could, but she had proved it was possible for a Deaf girl to get her groove on.

I tracked down the phone number of every dance studio in Tulsa, and called each one using a video relay service. I could use sign language, and the relay interpreter would voice my words aloud for the hearing person on the other end of the line, and also sign their responses back to me on the video I could see. Only one studio ended up taking my call: the Allstar Ballroom Dance Company.

Allstar was owned by the husband-and-wife dance team of Jon and Cassie Hamilton. They were so gracious and open to the challenge of teaching me. I spent a year in private lessons with Jon and a sign language interpreter, the three of us flying around the room together. Jon finally learned enough sign language, and I learned enough steps, that we didn't need an interpreter anymore, and I started going to all the ballroom dances I could find.

I had never been the athletic one, had never been one who could move comfortably in my body, and the integrative work of ballroom dance built in me such confidence. I did not have to be perfect at dancing. For the first time in my life I did not have to be perfect. It really does take two to tango, but I only had to be responsible for my part. I had to learn to trust, and let myself be led into that beauty that is spirit and body and music all wrapped up together.

Jon and Cassie became dear friends to me, but it gradually became clear that they were rather... different. I invited them to a housewarming party, and Cassie came but declined any alcohol. I just assumed she was in AA. They also had no smoking or alcohol permitted at their dance studio, which was unlike any of the others. There were subtler differences in the way they spoke, the way they dressed, and the way they interacted with each other and their children. There was an almost-visible light in them, and I wanted to know more.

They gave me a Book of Mormon for my birthday. I read it overnight. I slept all the next day, and read it again the next night, and again the next day. Everything changed.

It was the same gospel truths I had been taught growing up, except *more* somehow. There was a greater completeness, a fullness, a so-that's-what-it-means kind of feeling. It had threads of Isaiah, and I had always loved Isaiah, but it also had pieces which the Bible only seemed to imply: the beginning of things, the end of things, and the how-do-we-fix-this-mess things. There was redemption, with a clarity for which I had longed. After years of study, it was the first religion I had found whose truth was confirmed to me through prayer and direct revelation from the Holy Spirit, rather than dictated at me by others who said what I ought to believe.

The missionaries didn't oppress me with dogma. They told me they felt it was true, but that I could go and pray and ask God for myself. Instead of telling what to do, they taught me what covenants are. They taught me that temple covenants have the power to save families. They didn't try to tell me that men have a right to make choices for me. I would have kicked them right out of the door if they had. Instead, they told me I was eternal, and essential, and just like my Mother.

They told me it is never too late. They told me the atonement of Jesus Christ is big enough, even for me. That's when I began to cry. I understood the last twenty years of self-destruction could not be undone, but they were saying my life could be restored, that my family could be restored, and even that I could be restored. That was the hope that I needed, the hope of a prodigal daughter.

I tried their experiment. I prayed and I pondered. I tried implementing principles in my life, with baby steps of obedience. That was when my seed sprouted, and when I came alive again. I was still a mess, but I was alive, and I knew it.

I still didn't get baptized for a whole year almost, nine months like birthing the new baby that I was. There were many things I had to change, if I was going to be a covenant keeper. There were even people I had to let go of if I was going to be healthy and not sabotage myself. I was in a serious relationship at the time with a man who had a surprising amount of knowledge about my new church, The Church of Jesus Christ of Latter-day Saints, but he did not want to get baptized or get married, so I had to leave and start over once more.

My baptism day was a miracle for me, one that lifted the heaviness I had been carrying. It was a healing day that set me free. I felt as if I could suddenly see in color, even though I knew logically I was in the same world I had been in my whole life. The past seemed, for the first time, a million miles away, and I felt as if I had been lifted up out of filth, to stand clean on decent ground in my own right — not because of me, but because of the atonement. For the first time, I had been rescued instead of shamed, and helped instead of only condemned.

There is a story at the beginning of the Book of Mormon about a prophet who had a dream. He saw a tree with shining white fruit, symbols of the eternal life offered to us by our Father-in-Heaven. He wanted that fruit to be delicious to his family. He wanted his family to all be together, to be happy and healthy and well. That's how I felt after I was baptized. I knew I could not undo past choices, but I also knew forgiveness had been offered by One greater than myself, and that I had been promised restoration in some way.

But while restoration comes from above, restitution is still my part to do, and it is hard work. I had been estranged from my parents for years, so I started writing them every Sunday. I shared my testimony, thanked them for doing so much of our genealogy so that I could learn about our family, and told them about temples. My mother responded immediately.

My father responded once with an email, and told me he knew about the Mormons. It was a Mormon friend who had helped him do the genealogy, and he had considered learning more about the church at that time, but decided not to do so. Was it a coincidence that my parents got divorced soon after? My mother had a similar experience: we had lived next door to a Mormon family, and she learned some but decided not to pursue it. Not long after that was when I ran away and my brother moved to live with my dad. *But if there had been a scattering*, I thought, *then it must be true that there can also be a gathering*.

That thought gave me strength to keep trying with my mother, even though it was hard. Mothers are really good at pointing out what we do wrong, and that can be rough, because they have a greater vision than we do. But, mothers also forgive in a way no one else can, and my mother forgave me when no one else would.

One way we healed was through language, mine and hers. She loved word games, like *Take Two* and *Scrabble*, and would often leave me messages in letter tiles. Then she started learning sign language about the same time I got cochlear implants.

I wore hearing aids and didn't get cochlear implants until I was in my thirties. My hearing loss is a common degenerative genetic condition known as connexion 26 protein deficiency. It also impacted my balance, so I was very clumsy growing up and it took me a long time to learn to ride a bike. I only got desperate enough to ride on my own when my brother was going door to door selling popcorn. I wanted to go with him, but he told me training wheels were not allowed.

Getting cochlear implants was a big decision for me, both culturally and emotionally. It's still very controversial in Deaf culture, because Deaf people are proud of their deafness. It's our language, our community, our schools, and our history, and it is not something that needs curing. The other issue is that for many people, cochlear implants are the end of sign language. People see the cochlear implants on my head, and assume I can hear and understand them. Some audiologists even recommend against signing, so as not to interfere with learning to hear; this makes no sense, as if the eye doctor would tell my mom to stop speaking English just because she had Lasix surgery and didn't wear glasses anymore.

But for me and the context of my life, getting cochlear implants was the right decision. I did not have the benefit of growing up in Deaf schools. As an adult, I lived in a rural area where I had to fight for interpreters despite the law providing that right since before I was born. I worked as a counselor and chaplain with many hearing families who said they understood my need for an interpreter, but were reluctant to include an additional person in the room. I was weary of fighting for access that should have been automatic. I did want to keep my language of sign, but I also wanted more choices in accessibility. I still use and benefit from interpreters, and still sign, and will forever use captions when I watch movies. But the adventurer in me wanted to play in the world of sound, and my ticket was the cochlear implants. It was a very personal decision, and it cost me — between getting baptized and getting cochlear implants, I had few friends remaining by the end of that year.

Physically, it was scary to go through two major surgeries with no guarantee I would be able to hear. I tried to pray about being less afraid, but that would mean looking Him in the eye, and letting go of myself. It would mean daring to think I have a Father. It would mean accepting the fact that I am human. And weak. And overwhelmed.

"Do not be afraid," He whispered, "Move forward…"

I had learned that priesthood blessings were not just about laying hands on someone to help them, but about having the authority from God to do so. Anyone can comfort by reaching out to those in need, but there is power in having the *keys,* or permission and direction, to act as God's servant — like how my car only starts when "unlocked" by the proper key.

As a small act of faith, I requested a priesthood blessing from a father figure at church. He found a room for privacy, and pulled a chair out for me. I sat with my back up straight, my head bowed, and my arms folded reverently. He cleared his throat and stood behind me, resting his hands upon my head. After a moment of silence, he began to pronounce a blessing for me from Heavenly Father, one that promised strength and a return to health, but also one that promised my faith would grow through upcoming challenges. Heavenly Father said to me that He knew I wanted to move out of the dark place from which I had come, but that the only way to make that progress was through experience. He promised me one experience after another, like a frog jumping from one lily pad to the next, so that I might make progress at a miraculous rate. These would be difficult challenges, He said, and they would come quickly, but He promised that if I endured in faith, He would deliver me a successful surgery and a multiplicity of blessings.

There were two surgeries, first on the left side of my skull, and then on the right six months later, each followed by a painful recovery period. Since the auditory nerves are wrapped around the taste nerves, surgery both times left me with no sense of taste for over a year. Getting cochlear implants was challenging enough, but then came the really hard work.

For my implants to be successful, I had to practice with them all day, and couldn't cheat. To improve my voice, I had to wear a lapel microphone and listen to myself speak. I had to listen carefully and consciously, first to the silence between words, then the kinds of sounds that make up words, and then the weaving of words into sentences. The effort required was intense, and I understood why so many deaf adults quit before learning how to understand sound and its meaning.

I endured, though, and sound began to dance through me. My first trip to the symphony left me in awe and hungry for more. The bells in the percussion section are still the most distinct sounds I am able to hear, the clearest and crispest, like the flash of a camera. The other pieces of the orchestra are still blurry to me, just beyond what I can capture. The orchestra that night — oh! It was like voices in a conversation, different instruments talking back and forth to one another, pure and soft and lingering. It was, by far, the most powerful experience I have had outside of the Temple.

I kept reaching toward my head, almost unconsciously, because the music was so tangible to me. Before, music had been accessible to me only on paper, in some silent, visual, mathematical dance behind my eyes, or through touch, as I brushed the face of a speaker or felt crescendos through the floor. But this was an entirely different dimension. This was music that flowed into me and over me and through me, like a river of mist no one else could see.

Do you know what happens to a deaf child who doesn't learn language? They just sit there, or act out, or disappear inside themselves. They don't learn to read. They don't learn to express themselves. They don't know how to ask for what they need or want or prefer. They copy what everyone else does, whether it is good for them or not. They endure abuse, pain, suffering, and grief, without anyone telling them life could be different. They wait years to know the names of things, to describe how things are different, or to learn how to say their own name.

This was Mary's story. It knocked the breath out of me to see such beautiful brown ears, so silent and pure, on the same body as hands so still and quiet. There were no words in her fingers, not even simple ones, and it made me cry. She only had rough gestures and harsh sounds that felt like a hundred years ago, as if she had fallen through time and landed here begging for letters on her hands.

We already had signing in our home, and Alex and Anber loved teaching Mary the names of everything within reach the first night she came to us. They showed her around, and they were silly, and we ate pizza while I checked her thick, black, curly hair and washed her clothes. We got through baths, some serious ethnic hair combing, into pajamas, and ready for bed.

When we went to the green couch for family prayers, she knew to kneel down. I wondered who taught her to pray. She folded her hands together and closed her eyes, and just stayed there. The prayer ended and she didn't know to get up, because she couldn't hear the "Amen" and didn't know she could keep her eyes open and *see* the prayers at our house.

She held my hand as I walked her to her new bed. It was limp. Her hand was in mine, but she didn't hold my hand back. She let me hug her goodnight, but didn't hug back. She picked the top bunk, crawled up into a corner as far away from us as she could, and just laid there.

Mary told us she was deaf from being hit in the head by her father, who was now in prison. She was reportedly taken into custody on a night when her mother was stealing, even hiding items on her daughter. She also had prescription pills that were not hers, and a history of other petty crimes.

Mary's mother had denied Mary's hearing loss, despite the school's best efforts at getting her help. Mary had finally been fitted with hearing aids shortly before coming to us from another foster family that was uncomfortable caring for a deaf child. We taught Mary how to care for her hearing aids and helped make sure she was wearing them. We also put her back in kindergarten again, since she hadn't heard anything the first time around, and later sent her to Oklahoma School for the Deaf for first grade and sign language immersion.

She started responding to the world around her, and eagerly begged for the names of things and the sounds she heard. We taught her everything in both voice and sign, and her world expanded as she began to develop language.

Mary was aware that her biological mother was not improving.

"Mama, my other mom is still stealing stuff."

"I know, sweetie."

"And she still takes those pills."

"I know, sweetie."

"And she isn't very much of a grown up."

This I knew. When Mary got a LeapPad system for Christmas, her mother wore out the battery before Mary ever got to play with it. When they had their weekly, one-hour supervised visit, her mother would color the coloring books before giving them to her daughter. Mary would come home from visits saying that her mother had been kicked out again, was homeless again, or got fired for stealing again.

Mary's relationship with her mother was tricky in other ways as well. One morning we were fixing her hair, and she randomly piped up with, "Someone is going to have to tell my mom that I'm not white." It was true! Her mother even insisted to my face, after undoing the braids that had taken me hours to put in Mary's hair, that her daughter was not black. Mary was now old enough to know this wasn't accurate, and to be bothered by it.

Mary knew that Alex and Anber were getting adopted, and that they were getting a lot of attention for it. We sensed that a showdown was brewing. It started with lunch, simply enough. She had been fussy and bossy all day, but nothing out of the ordinary for our six-year-old extrovert. Each of the children picked what they wanted to eat, and no one complained even when they had to have a fruit and some vegetables with it. Mary quickly chose an apple, and skipped to the table happily enough.

Nothing seemed amiss until she took a little fairy bite out of just the skin, and loudly announced she was "done" because she had "tried a bite".

"No," I said, "you chose the apple, so you need to go ahead and eat it."

She looked me right in the eyes, picked up her apple, reached over, and dropped it on the floor. On purpose. Daring me to do something about it as she turned back to start eating the fun part of her meal.

Our teenager in residence at the time, who often forgot she wasn't the mom, reminded Mary she needed to finish her vegetables. Mary replied by looking me in the eyes again, picking up her vegetables one by one, and flicking them onto the floor.

We do not have finish-your-plate rules at our house. It's common for foster children to come with food issues, and we never force any of them to eat. No one gets dessert, however, without eating the nutritious parts first, which usually motivates those who are merely picky eaters.

This defiance of all the manners Alex had carefully practiced over the past two years was too much for him, and he suddenly shouted out, "I can't believe you are throwing food on the floor! That is so gross! You better tell mom you are sorry!"

Always ready to join any fight, Anber chimed in with, "Yeah, you pick those up! You eat those dirty foods on the floor!"

Before I could respond to their bullying behavior, Mary began to scream.

She screamed like I had never seen her scream. Her scream was like an Anber scream, like the entire ocean of emotions inside her was going to come out. She screamed like she suddenly felt the weight of grief from her mother's poor choices, the loss of her home and family, the confusion at why two other children could be adopted already and not her yet, and the irritation at not being an only child anymore. All of it welled up in her in some kind of emotional tsunami, and came out of her in a feral wail.

This was naturally followed by an all-out temper tantrum on the floor, kicking and screaming right there under the table, carrots and broccoli flying in the air while the apple rolled somewhere under the couch. I stayed calm and reached for her hands, and initially she responded to me. We got part-way through the kitchen toward her room, when the wave of emotions turned into rage, and she turned on me. Her hearing aids and my cochlear implants went flying as she launched into a wild panther leap toward me, but her socked feet slipped from under her, knocking me over, and she fell in a pile on the floor. I got her picked up again and walked her to her room, where she lay crying for some time.

When she was quiet, I went to open her door. I told her she could stay there and rest if she wanted, but if she was hungry she could go pick up her vegetables and finish her apple (which had been found uncontaminated on a coloring book).

This is our Mary, who holds things in for so long that nothing comes out until it all boils over at once. She had so many things she was sad about, and so many things she was angry about, and so many things hurting her. None of it was about lunch, or the apple, or tossed vegetables. It was about her biological mother, who was very nearly younger than Mary developmentally. Her mother, who couldn't stop abusing substances long enough to win Mary back. Her mother, who couldn't get a job because she couldn't stop stealing. It was about a father she could barely remember and didn't know at all. It was about a whole side of her family that she needed to teach her what black means. It was about her grandfather, whom Mary loved but was also afraid of because of the hostile way he treated her mother. Her grandfather, who, for reasons of age and temperament, was unwilling to adopt her. This girl, who wanted so badly to be adopted but also to return to live with her mother, grieved for the loss of a family that didn't seem to want her.

I made sure, when it was bed time, to spend extra cuddle time with Mary that night. We tickled and snuggled and wriggled around laughing until I knew she was okay again, until she knew she was okay again. It's a lot to process for such little ones, and hard to do so when we don't actually have any answers for anything. The only answer I have to give is to keep loving and to keep trying. That's all we have to give, sometimes.

Mary's worker stopped by unexpectedly one afternoon, to warn us that Mary's biological mother had not only made no progress at all, but was actually worse off than when she had started. The law had changed, she said, and the grace period before termination of parental rights had been moved from fifteen months to six months, and the District Attorney (DA) already wanted to file. She told us we needed to be ready with an answer, whether we would be willing to adopt Mary or not, or at least keep her long term if she did not want to be adopted.

How could we send her away? Of course she could stay. But the interminable process of finalizing Alex and

Anber's adoptions had taught us not to get too excited about things just yet. We never knew what would actually go down in court. Besides, termination of parental rights is never something to celebrate. It's a grief, a sadness, an acknowledgment of trauma and neglect and hard things already endured. Maybe it's okay to be relieved, because it means the child will be safe, but it's not party time when a family ends.

It was during this period of legal limbo that Mary was prescribed cochlear implants, and her mother signed consents for her to have the surgeries. I had always wondered whether or not I would choose cochlear implants for a child of mine, but she was not ours and surgery was not our choice. I spoke with her a great deal, though, about sign language and her need to continue signing no matter how well she could hear. She looked at my processors and asked many questions. I told her that if she learned both worlds, she could choose her accessibility options for herself when she was older, but first she must learn both to hear and to sign.

Mary asked for a priesthood blessing, and it made me happy to know she understood the comfort and guidance that can come from such sacred encounters with God. She dressed in her purple and green pajamas that she wanted to wear to the hospital the next morning, and I braided her hair with ribbons. She climbed into a chair in the living room, and the children and I sat on the couches, surrounding her with love. Nathan stood behind her, placed his hands on her head, and gave her a blessing. The words were not only of healing from the surgery, but of comfort for the grieving the loss of her mother that she loved so much but who was unable to choose her back. We all cried that night, and we snuggled with her for a long time before tucking her into bed.

This moment, like the blessing before my own surgery, was one of the many experiences that helped me to understand that the priesthood was not something men held like a possession, but a role they played on behalf of my Heavenly Father. I had also realized my own role in the priesthood, as established in our family, in that I could call down the power of Heaven through prayer and by setting the tone of our home like a Temple, even while my husband delivered the blessing itself. We worked together in this way, each of us with unique roles in the council and guidance of our family as we gathered them.

This was a big moment for us as we took one of our children into surgery for the first time. We had to wake early, needing to be at the hospital by six in the morning with an hour's drive ahead of us. Her mother was back in jail when it came time for surgery, so we took her alone. Mary played with mazes on the wall while I checked her in at the admissions desk, and watched *Doc McStuffins* while waiting for her turn in the operating room. I used a Sharpie to write "Rock On" behind the ear, so that the surgeon would laugh when he saw it.

I was more emotional than expected when they wheeled her away from me, crying as her little hand held up the "ILY" sign for *I love you* until she was out of sight. My heart was heavy with worry to have such a little one in surgery, and my mind was spinning in circles over whether or not cochlear implants were the right thing for her. I held on to the words of her blessing, though, that she would do well as she learned to hear, and that hearing would help her in new ways we had not yet imagined.

Mary was not impressed with the pain when she woke up, and less impressed with the white bandage wrapped around her head. I had warned her of all this, and that I myself had not been able to move my head for several weeks following my surgeries. However, surgery didn't seem to faze her, and I had to pull her down from the jungle gym twice the next day.

That girl who originally was so flat and sad now brightens the room with contagious laughter, and that girl they said was cognitively delayed with no language is the smartest kid in her class. And as the oldest girl in our home, she is definitely the boss of the family, and in charge of declaring what is and is not cool.

Before I was baptized, I didn't understand priesthood authority, priesthood keys, or why there is a difference between how men and women access this power. But having watched it in action in my life and in the lives of my children, I have begun to see the harmony of it all. My husband teaches our children violin lessons; I teach them piano. Together, we teach them music.

Whether it is the men "holding" the priesthood by what they do, or women "being" the priesthood by who we are, the point is to serve God's children and build His kingdom. It changes me, making me more of who I was designed to be by aligning me with God, and giving me a power greater than my own with which to love and care for those around me. Like Mary's blessing, the priesthood is for families: spoken by the mouth of a humble priesthood servant, fortified by a mother's powerful prayers, and received by a precious, faithful daughter of God.

# 5

Once the caseworker had gotten parental consents and wrangled pre-approval from Medicaid, this two-month-old little girl who couldn't breathe was scheduled for a week of testing that would exhaust any adult: Monday would be an anesthesia consult, Tuesday would be GI and pulmonary, Wednesday would be in the operating room for tests and scopes, Thursday would be a sleep study overnight, and Friday would be swallow studies and X-rays. There would be a microlaryngoscopy, flexible bronchoscopy, upper endoscopy, video swallow study, fiber optic endoscopic evaluation of swallowing (FEES), a CT of the face, and a consultation with plastic surgery to evaluate for a likely mandibular distraction.

The nurse was very patient with me on the phone and by email, explaining all of this several times so that I would understand what was happening. I knew what X-rays were. I also thought a CT scan seemed simple until I realized this baby was not going to be happy about being strapped down to a moving table. The anesthesia consult and scope tests were scary, because she would have to be intubated in the operating room with a breathing tube, and her airway was too small for that to be easy. Scarier still was extubation, because of how the trachea swells shut when the tubes are removed. Her airway had no extra room for any swelling, which could easily leave her in crisis, with the doctors unable to re-intubate her in an emergency.

The most fascinating tests to watch were the swallow studies. They put barium in her formula, and fed her while taking pictures and video of what happened as she swallowed. We could see how her tongue moved at the tip and at the base, how the milk went up into her palate and came down again, and how it bounced off throat as it went down — right into her lungs. This is called aspiration, and caused her to have pneumonia frequently. We could hear her cough and choke when she aspirated sometimes, but other times it was "silent" and we had no idea it was happening. We could see that it would actually have been worse had her airway not been the size of a coffee stirring straw, because liquids had trouble getting passed that small opening. In that way, her small airway was protective in some respect.

The test that took the longest that week was the overnight sleep study. This was in a room that looked like a normal hospital room, except that there were video cameras on the bed and computers by the wall. I had to take off her preemie pajamas, and they spent an hour gluing electrodes on her chest, face, and in the hair on her head. They taped over the glue, pulling the electrode wires out into colored groups. There was not an inch of her face or head that didn't have a little metal disc glued down, and I fed her to keep her still during the torture. They strapped monitors to her toes and feet and around her belly and chest, and then I put her pajamas back on over them so she wouldn't pull them off. I swaddled her, but wasn't allowed to pick her up, so I tried patting her on the bottom to lull her to sleep as she lay face down on the bed. I hung a blanket on the side of her crib to try and block some of the light from the computers, and used an app on my iPad to play water sounds to drown out the monitor beeps. This also helped block out the sound of the sleep study nurses, who came in and out all night, measuring and adjusting and checking on things.

She was mad as anything by morning, and wanted those electrodes off. They soaked them in something that smelled worse than nail polish, and slipped them off as fast as they could while she screamed at them. She was covered in slime and sticky glue, and they told us dish soap would be the best way to get it out of her hair. It took three more baths to get her clean, and we were both glad to finally make it back to her room on the airway unit to get some rest.

When we got there, a nurse was waiting to ask me for help with consents for surgery. When you are a foster parent, you have no rights to consent to surgery. In some states, it is the child's caseworker that consents to surgery, meaning that the worker can sign all the paperwork. In our state, foster parents can sign consents for outpatient services, caseworkers can sign for things that are more intrusive, like blood draws, but biological parents have to give consent for anything requiring anesthesia.

The baby's caseworker had signed all the consents for the testing before we came, and had gotten signatures for the scopes. But depending on her test results, there would be more surgery to come, and now they needed new consents. The baby's biological mother was in jail again, and the nurses were having to call the jail to talk to the chaplain, who was the only one who was authorized to get the mother out of her cell to talk on the phone. They had to wait for him to get her, and then for the chaplain to call back. It was a mess, and taking ages. When they finally got in touch with her, she gave her consent to surgery... but not for anesthesia. I wanted to shout, *Who does that?!*

Some babies have congenital challenges, and no one knows why it happens to one baby and not the next. That's hard enough. But what if those problems are because her mother used drugs the entire pregnancy, or from abuse or neglect? It's a slippery slope, thinking of all the ways to blame someone for the past, instead of dealing with the present.

It would be different if we were adopting a new baby from a birth mother who had chosen adoption. We would pick her out, and she would be an amazing woman who was brave and good, sacrificing to care for both herself and her child as best she could. She would choose as well, knowing we're a little bit quirky and artist-ish, with a mom who writes nerdy essays and psychoanalyzes people all day while the dad writes musicals and flies all over the country for his productions. We would talk about our resumes of parenting life, how we believe in reading aloud, and eating fresh vegetables, and that we have a strong faith that teaches us to love people instead of condemning them. We would tell her our hobbies of music and cooking and dancing and cozy restaurants and culture and travel. At least, we would hope she'd learn all that, somehow spotting our profile among the thousands of other prospective parents.

Instead, we signed up for fostering, long before our miscarriages happened, and that's how we got the job of taking care of other people's children. We took in whatever kiddos needed a place to live. The parents never got to pick us out, so they never had much reason to believe in us. Instead of making a courageous and honorable choice, these were parents who made mistakes, so it was sometimes hard for us to believe in them. But we tried because we believe in families, even when they didn't believe in us.

No one performs the miracle of bringing those little ones into the world except those birth parents, and that is to be honored always. We are thankful for them on Thanksgiving, and light candles for them on Christmas, and make gifts for mailing on Mother's Day and Father's Day. We even still have visits with some family, when it is safe for all of us and the children choose to see them. We take pictures of birthdays and save schoolwork and make little handprint gifts to send when we can.

That's what happened with Alex. We saved all his schoolwork, and all his pictures, and all the funny quotes of the hilarious things he said, but his parents never took the steps required for reunification. He became ours without them, which is different than being theirs and also ours, together.

Adopting through foster care is different than any other kind of adoption because the parents are usually not giving up their children voluntarily. Regardless of the circumstances or conditions which led to their children being removed from their care, the parents only understand that the children were lost. Taken. Stolen.

I had begun struggling with that layer as Alex's adoption came up, just before the baby first came home from the hospital in Oklahoma City. I saw his mother in court for the first and what seemed like probably the last time, and I didn't know what to say to her. She had not been to any of the other hearings, and I didn't know if she was just not functioning well enough to come to court, or if she wanted to lose rights so that Alex could have a different life, or if she just didn't care.

If she were a birth mother choosing to give up her child for adoption, there would be more to say. There would be more she would want to know. She would ask about the child. We could be friends, even if it stung, and we would be bonded together in our loving of the child, even if we did not fully understand that relationship during this lifetime. There would be compassion. There would be appreciation.

But this was not that story. She didn't ask how he was doing, and didn't look through the pile of papers I had saved for her. I didn't know what to say, but I did want to have compassion. Over the following weeks, I drafted several letters to her, but crumpled them one after another.

*My husband and I have had five miscarriages, and know a taste of the grief of losing a child. I know that's not the same as the pain you feel now. I am sorry that it hurts, and cannot imagine how much it hurts. We will be forever grateful for this gift of a child you have given us. He is a miracle to us. We will always tell him you love him, and will remind him of the good stories of you we know. We will tell him he has your red hair, and that he is tall like his father. We will tell him he has your nose, and his father's lips, and your toes. We will tell him we got to hug you, that you said you love him, and that we all cried together.*

My first draft was too self-centered, and by the end of it I still couldn't find the words to make the situation better or easier.

*We didn't plan on adopting. Even fostering was a surprise to us, but we certainly didn't plan on adopting. But fostering happened, and in fact, your son was the first one who stayed.*

I crumpled up that paper into a ball, and tossed it into the trash.

*Where have you been for nine months? Why haven't you or your husband done anything the court asked? How can you just not even try? Do you not want to know anything about him?*

Crumple again.

*I saved you all his papers from school. Every single one.*

Crumple.

*I want to thank you.*

Crumple.

*I am really sorry.*

Crumple.

*I can't imagine what today feels like for you.*

Crumple.

*We are so excited that…*

Crumple.

*We really love him.*

Crumple.

In the end, there were no words, and I simply gave her a photo book of all the pictures we had taken in those two years he had lived with us. There were pictures of his birthdays, and Christmases, and New Year's Days. Pictures of him learning to ride a bike, learning to write, and learning to read. Pictures of him getting his long curls cut off, and pictures of him playing soccer. Alex on his first day of school, on family vacations, and smiling in his Sunday best at the temple in Oklahoma City. Every picture of him got squeezed into that book.

I also struggled through similar feelings with Anber's mother. *How could you?* smashed right up against *My heart aches for you.* These emotions exploded when we found out she was pregnant with a second child, but still using heroin and other drugs. Every time she got arrested, she tested positive once more. I had so many things to say to her:

*We have worked with many parents, whose children have come and gone. They talked to us, and worked hard, and we enjoyed the friendships that came from sharing a purpose, even when those friendships were challenged as children went back and forth between us. But it was always about the children. That's why they got their children back.*

*When you stop replying to me, that's when I know you have relapsed again. When your phone starts showing messages delivered but not read, that's when I know you have been arrested again. I pray for you anyway, but I pray extra then, and I hope I am wrong. I need to be wrong. I need you to be well.*

*But there you are, in the daily police report, in a different county now, arrested again, with more DUI charges, more drug possession, more substances in your body that is supposed to be growing a baby. I am not here to argue with you about whose baby it is. There is nothing either of us can do to change that, and it is something you chose long ago. The baby is a child of God, and not a possession or the latest fashion accessory or a Happy Meal toy.*

*I did not take your child from you, and have nothing to do with the process of you getting her back. The child with me has been in my home for a year and a half, and grown from an infant to a toddler, and is quickly becoming a preschooler. She has your temper, your fierce anger at the world, and a terrifying anxiety about whether the world will be safe for her or not. She scowls at strangers, and wails when we leave her at bedtime, or at preschool, or in the church nursery, because you didn't always come back. She is long and thin like you, but she has, in my opinion, her father's features, with her big eyes and broad forehead. The serious expression she carries is his, even if you say you don't know who he is. I have seen him, and I see him in your daughter.*

*This new baby you carry inside you has endured as much already, and isn't even born yet. Not even born, but for seven months so far has taken meth every time you have, has shot up heroin every time you have, and has passed out from alcohol and narcotics every time you have. Sometimes, when I hear stories about your substance abuse, or read the reports of all your arrests since last summer, I wonder if the baby is even going to be born alive. And if it is born alive, how many months the baby will scream and cry while withdrawals rack* its tiny little body, how long before we know what damage has been done to its developing brain? How long before some "normal" high school exposure to recreational drugs ends in disaster because of the addiction training you are giving it now? If the baby lives that long.

I am so angry with you. I cannot even say how angry I am. It seems wrong, on the surface, that life should happen in such a way that some couples try so hard to have and raise a family so carefully, and others lose them so carelessly. It is an injustice that these tiny babies would start out with so much against them.

Except also I am so sad for you, because I am watching you lose everything: first your infant, then your apartment, then your job, then your man, then your freedom, and now soon this new baby. I cannot imagine the depth of your sorrow.

I did not think about the grief you must be feeling until I saw you cry the second time we met in court. The first time you did not cry, because you were so high and aggressive and tried to get in an actual fight with the judge. You didn't ask about your baby that day.

I do remember the day you did ask, though, the day we sat in the sun and talked about your daughter. I remember who you were when you were clean and sober, and how much you loved your baby those days. I will tell her the story of it, and I promise she will always know that part of the story. You did love her. Loving her was never part of the crisis. You love her still, somewhere in you, I know.

The crisis was always heroin. Track marks in your hands and feet. Stealing trucks and trying to run over your boyfriend. Pulling a knife on your sister. Pushing your mom out of a car while she was driving. Trying to take a gun from *a police officer. Shoplifting. So much lying, so much stealing. Heroin, heroin, heroin. Heroin made you some kind of monster, a completely different creature from the timid and attentive person I saw you to be those few days you were clean and sober.*

*I will tell Anber about that day, always, and tell this baby, too, if this one comes to stay with us. I am not your therapist, and you rarely let me be your friend, so I can only piece together why you chose what you chose. Maybe you had been so hurt for so long, you just wanted to turn it all off? Maybe real life was too boring and under-stimulating for you, and so you just wanted to up the volume on everything? Maybe you chose the wrong friends, or they found you? I suspect that, besides your own trauma, you may also be bi-polar. Maybe you were self-medicating?*

*Please, stop doing heroin. Just stop. There are so many ways to feel better, so many resources to help, so many people who really do care about you. Except I don't know that you can stop. I am afraid heroin has stolen you away.*

*I do not claim to know your life, but I have lived a hard one, too. I have had my own years of being destructive. Really. But it's okay to leave trauma-drama alongside the road when you wash at the river, and to keep walking without picking it up again. I know this, and I know you are not alone. We are not alone.*

*They say they are going to take your new baby from you when it is born. I cry tears at this: for relief that the baby will be safe, for grief for you, for my own grief and knowing the loss of a baby you cannot raise, for joy that Anber may get to grow up with her sibling, for fear that the baby won't get to grow up, and for sorrow that these are the consequences playing out.*

*Anber knows you are back in jail, because she asked. She knows the baby will be born in jail, and that we don't know if the baby will be alive or not. She doesn't know everything, but she knows the things a two-year-old can understand. Your daughter prays for you. I want you to know that.*

While fostering, our job was to support families and mentor biological parents, acting as a bridge to support reunification. But when they burned those bridges, it became more challenging to remain connected and supportive. As long as the biological parents took any steps at all to correct the conditions that resulted in the removal of the child — even just making an appointment, or cleaning their house, or scheduling a parenting class — they got more time to keep trying, month after month. But when the parents made no progress at all, refusing any help from caseworkers while rejecting the support we offered, there was little anyone could do.

A year and a half after Alex first came to live with us, the state finally filed a motion for termination of parental rights. When that happens, parents are given a choice. They can voluntarily relinquish their rights, sometimes earning special favor from criminal court, or they can do nothing, and lose their rights automatically, or they can demand a jury trial — not to determine whether the child should be returned, but whether the parent should have more time to fix things.

Alex's mother, holding on tight to a precious book of photos, heard these choices in the one court hearing she attended. She had to return for the next hearing to formally declare her choice, but she simply did not show up and her rights were terminated by default.

His father, however, demanded a trial. The trial would not be a custody battle about whether he or we were the better parents; it would only address the father's initial charges and determine whether he had resolved those conditions that had caused Alex to be taken into custody in the first place. Alex really loved his biological father, because he was his father, regardless of how much he wanted to be adopted or what his father had done. It just was, and it made trial week be a yucky experience for Alex, either way. No matter what happened, he would grieve.

Alex was subpoenaed as a witness. We dressed him up in his size six suit, with a brand new Spider-Man bow tie. We fortified him with a lunch of chicken nuggets, and then went to the victim's room in the courthouse to begin the wait. About the time he finished playing with every toy available, they finally came to say that Alex would testify next, and so to get ready. He held on to me tightly, with a stuffed frog in the other hand, as we walked down the back hallway to the courtroom. The doors opened, and they called his name. I was not allowed in with him.

*Trust me*, I heard my Father whisper to me.

When Alex came out, his face was red and splotchy. Clutching the frog, he pushed through doors, and sank into me. The attorney would only tell me, "Alex said everything." I didn't know what that meant.

*Trust me*, I heard my Father say.

The attorney left. My heart was pounding and I hadn't breathed in hours. I sat alone in the jury room holding Alex close, no idea what they really asked him or what he said. He was quiet a long time, before looking up and saying, "They asked me about when I lived with my other dad, and I told them I want to live with him again because he is my dad and his bad choices aren't my fault and God loves all of us and I just want a family forever." He broke down crying, and so did I.

I carried him out to the car like the toddler he was when he first came. I tucked him in his seat, put on his favorite music, and sat there to breathe a minute so that I could drive home. I had no idea if he really said that to the jury or not, or, if he did, what that would mean or what would happen.

The next morning, I moved slowly getting ready for the last day of court, when it was my turn to testify. I came out of my room ready to grab babies to drop off at preschool on my way, but everything fell apart when we realized that somehow we had forgotten it was the most dreaded day of the entire school year: Valentine's Day.

Long gone were the idyllic dreams of how we would always make homemade cards, and send clever gifts instead of fake, sugar-addiction candy. Long gone was our free time to browse Pinterest for ideas to celebrate this holiday of love. The morning became a mad rush of kindergarten signatures and preschool scribbles on mass-produced cards, with no one in a hurry except us parents. The light-hearted notes full of lame jokes seemed ironic on such a dramatic day. We finished just in time to leave for school, only to discover our kindergartners had not worked on homework sheets since before the trial started, and worse, none of us knew what it meant to decompose 13 in the new Common Core curriculum.

We finally zipped up the last coat, and got all the car seats buckled, and said a family prayer right there in the car. Nathan pulled out to take the children to breakfast at school, and I started the hour long drive to the courthouse. It already felt like lifetimes had passed since court the day before.

I tried to stay calm, always remembering to be extra careful on the road because of what happened to my mom. I could feel my blood pressure going up, and I had to consciously calm myself back down. I had no words left to pray, though I was in a prayerful state, and so I listened to some cello music. This was exactly what I needed, and by the time I got to the courthouse, I could feel the prayers of so many loved ones resting upon me in a tangible way. Filled with the deepest peace and calm, I walked in to that courthouse fully alert, fully confident, and fully me.

I checked in at the DA's office, and got whisked back to prep with the District Attorney and Alex's attorney. They told me that they didn't want to put too much pressure on me, but that I needed to be their star witness. They said to remember I was testifying as a foster mom, but that I am a foster mom with a doctorate and twenty years of experience as a counselor. They said they needed me to stay on topic, and answer the other attorney as concisely as possible, but to still be myself.

We were the only two witnesses left, they said, just me and then Alex's father.

I was up first.

I can't write anything else about what happened in the court room, of course. But here is what I can tell you: I saw the hand of God that morning. I really did. The DA and Alex's attorney were both able to pull out of me an accurate picture of Alex, his interactions with his father, how he had grown, and how he fit into our family now. It felt good and right and complete and whole, and there was nothing I felt that was left out or misinterpreted.

When I got cross-examined, it was like swinging a bat at fireballs, but I never got scared and I never flinched and I never missed. There was one time I misunderstood a question, but I was able to get it answered without being trapped. I watched the hand of God reveal light and truth, and swirl things around until everything landed in the right place. I was in awe that such worship could happen from the stand in a court room. I will never forget it.

After I stepped down, Alex's father got called up. Because I had already testified, they now let me stay in the court room to listen and watch. The attorneys were incredible. They brought all their arguments and evidence together in a moment of clarity so perfect that even Alex's father seemed to understand what was coming — and then the judge called lunch, just like that. It was like on TV, where right as they build to a dramatic revelation, they cut to commercial. It was almost like the judge emphasized that moment, by pulling everyone out of their trance and back into real life. And it meant the jury sat pondering that moment all through lunch.

After the break, I went back for the last of Alex's father's testimony, but it was difficult to sit and listen to it. The defense attorney's arguments fell apart, and when the DA got up to cross-examine, she nailed it. She called out all the holes in the defense, and then brought out even more history I hadn't known about before. I felt sad for his father, and everyone felt uncomfortable.

When the jury came back from deliberation, the verdict was read aloud in the courtroom. The jury declared him guilty on the original charges, as well as in failing to correct those conditions. Parental rights were terminated.

*We got Alex!* The jury was excused, and every one of them came up and shook my hand to thank me for what we had done for him. I just stood there and cried.

When Alex's father was dismissed from the courtroom, he raised his hand and asked if he could say one more thing. The judge let him, warning him the trial was over and he was off the record. Alex's father said, "It's okay. This is just for me, and just public. I just want to apologize for what I did, and have done, and didn't do. I know it was wrong, and I take full responsibility. I wanted to apologize for that, and for wasting your time this week. I knew I couldn't win this trial, but trying was the last and only way I could show my son that I really love him, even though I messed up so bad. So I had to do it, and you gave me a fair trial, and I wanted to thank you."

He hung his head and turned to leave, walking quietly toward the back of the courtroom. I ran up and hugged him full on, as tight as I could. He is a tall man, just under seven feet tall, and thin as a rail, and I just swallowed him up in my arms, crying with him. We stood there like that, for a long time. He said, "Thank you for teaching him that I do love him, and I am sorry for what I have done. Keep praying with him, and take him to church, because that's all that can save us now."

"I promise," I said.

And then he walked out.

And just like that, we had a son.

When we got home, we set up a movie for the children, and then pulled Alex aside to talk to him. "The judge and jury have finished their work," I explained, "and they decided two things. They decided a sad thing and a happy thing.

"The sad thing is that they said your other dad cannot be your parent anymore, even though he will always be your first daddy and love you no matter what." Nathan and I were ready to console him, to give him time and space, and to deal with some behavioral acting out. Except that's not what happened.

As soon as I gave him the sad news, Alex jumped up and screamed, "That means I am getting adopted! Whoo-hoo!" He jumped on me with a bear hug so big it knocked me over on the floor, and he started laughing and squealing, and screamed for Anber to come. She ran in, and he shouted again, "I am getting adopted!" They started cheering, and jumping up and down and laughing, screaming "Adopted! Adopted!" over and over and over, while climbing over me and Nathan. I just laid there and cried and cried and cried.

It was only a few weeks later when Anber's jury trial was announced. The court date was set for after the new baby was due to be born, which would make the sibling a part of Anber's case. If the mother's rights were terminated, she would be losing two children instead of one. I don't know if someone explained this to Anber's mother, or if she figured it out, or if it was coincidence, but two weeks before the baby was born, Anber's mother signed to relinquish her rights voluntarily. Anber was ours without a fight.

This timing separated Anber from the baby's case, leaving everyone scrambling to figure out who had jurisdiction over her when she was born. It also meant the newborn baby girl, with who-knows-what-kind-of-challenges, would be left alone at the hospital when her mother was transported back to jail. After experiencing Anber's struggles with attachment, we were especially anxious to get there somehow, to hold her and give her the best start we could under terrible circumstances.

This new baby girl was the only one of our foster children of whom we were aware throughout the pregnancy. She was the only baby who came home with us from the hospital and stayed. And in spite of the legal hurdles, and the unthinkable medical traumas that loomed ahead, she was the only baby whom I got to see on the day she was born. This baby, our baby, was born dead in jail, and I was the chaplain on call when the ambulance brought her to the hospital, but it would be two more months before we could bring her home.

# 6

We spent half of every day in Cincinnati enduring one hard thing after another. We spent the other half quietly playing or singing together. She curled up in my arms for hours, our eyes locked together, keeping each other safe so far from Oklahoma. It was precious time, in the midst of such crisis, that we would not have had together in the chaos of everyday life back home. That Life Flight had lifted me from the busy, working-mom world, to a place where watching my baby sleep was time well spent.

Of course, watching her sleep was more than just new mother love. It meant tracking the numbers on her monitors, and listening to the tornado rumble that came from her throat as she tried to breathe. It meant staying awake so that she stayed alive long enough for the next surgery that would save this miracle baby's life. Again.

It was surgery day. Her medical team told me to expect her to be under anesthesia for a few hours. The best case scenario was that she would be back up to our room before lunch. Worst case scenario, her heart would struggle enough that we would need to move up to Pediatric Intensive Care Unit (PICU).

I wanted the baby to have a bath, because I knew it would be a while before she got another one. We

untangled the outfit I had forced over her IV's, and laid
it aside as she wriggled around to watch me. A nurse
and I filled a small pink tub halfway, mixing in baby
shampoo just enough to build a few suds. I took a white
cloth and dipped it in the warm water, lifting it to
squeeze out the excess. The nurse helped hold the baby
in a position in which she could breathe while I washed
her tiny limbs, her too-small chest, and smooth back.
The baby smiled at the warm cloth each time I pressed
it to her, but then wailed when I lifted it away and the
cold air hit her skin. We wrapped her in a bright white
towel once she was clean, changing out the water to
rinse her off again.

Her huge, bright blue eyes made her enchanting to
look at, but the misshapen part of her face made her
difficult to see. It wasn't so much that her small lower
jaw made her any less beautiful, but more that your
mind got stuck trying to figure out why she didn't have
a chin, the way an old record skips when it is scratched.
From the profile, her face was perfectly formed from the
top of her forehead and down to her nose, but then at
her lips, the angle jarred suddenly the wrong way,
turning sharply toward her neck where her lower jaw
and chin should have been. Her half-Pakistani hair was
long and thick and black, though, and curled around her
face almost hiding this from view.

Just as we tied a hospital gown around her, a tech
arrived to lead us to the surgery suite. She pushed the
baby's bed, but told me that I could carry her all the way
to anesthesia. I soaked in every sensation of holding her
close to my heart. We needed this surgery to keep her
alive, but there was no knowing if she would pull
through or not. If she did, she would have a great battle

of pain ahead of her, and it was a terrifying thing to intentionally carry her toward such a trial. A woman wearing the now-familiar blue outfit of surgical scrubs met me outside the anesthesia room, lifted the baby from my arms, and carried her away from me.

She was gone only an hour before I was paged to the waiting area desk. I needed to pack our things and move to the PICU. That was all the information I got. I pushed the elevator buttons with shaking hands. In the halls, I couldn't look anyone in the eye. Coming back to the room without her felt like a hole in my heart — a hole I was far too familiar with already.

It was three more hours before I was able to meet with a doctor in the consultation room. He cleared his throat, and was staring at me. I was not sure how long I had been away in my own head, trying to process... for seconds, maybe, or years. *She is alive. But she is alive. That's good, right? She is alive!*

"Do you understand what I am telling you? Do you have any questions?"

*I am a chaplain,* I say. *I understand.*

I wondered if this was why I had to become a chaplain, so that I would understand. I needed to stay in my head because there was no private space in the whole hospital for me to cry. This news I had been waiting for, I did not want.

She was alive and fighting hard, but it was such a struggle. Our sweet little baby, whose giant eyes were once bright with life and hope, was now on life support. The surgery was nearly too much for her, her struggling heart, and her limited airway. There was a problem trying to intubate her. There was a problem with her heart during surgery. Fluids. Lungs. Congestive heart failure. This. That. Also this. Also that. And now she was in a coma, being kept alive by a machine.

They said if she tried to wake up before morning, they would put her back in a coma intentionally. From a medical trauma coma on accident, to a medically induced coma on purpose. Because she needed to stabilize her airway and her heart. Because other scary things could happen, like strokes or medical cerebral palsy or death. Or all three.

So, the good news: the surgery itself was a brilliant success, if she could pull through. The bad news, of course: coma. The worst news didn't emerge until later. Did it make sense, with the baby being completely unconscious, that giant tears were rolling down from her closed eyes? The doctors leapt into action, and soon realized that there was nothing protecting this little girl from the pain of the four metal bars that had just been inserted into her jaws.

Because her mother had used so many drugs during pregnancy, she had given her baby a tolerance to pain killers beyond the level of safe infant doses. They could not give her any more morphine without stopping her heart. They finally found a combo of two alternative drugs in a high-dose drip that worked well enough to stop the tears, but they could tell the pain continued, adding further stress to her innocent heart, already beating too hard too fast.

I had been the chaplain on call at the hospital in Tulsa when the ambulance screeched up to the emergency room. The code blue set off my pager, alerting me to a life or death emergency, and I raced to meet the response team. They were transferring a newborn from the ambulance to the Neonatal Intensive Care Unit (NICU), and I was surprised to see that she was on her belly instead of her back. She was still on bagged air, and the EMTs reported that this miracle baby had already been resuscitated several times en route.

She was so tiny that she fit in my hands. Her spirit was beautiful and perfect, but her body revealed one challenge after another as they cleaned her up and tried to keep her breathing. *No chin. Small jaw bones. No tongue. Cleft palate. Missing sinus structures. Abnormal skull and facial bones. Respiratory distress. Noxious substance affecting newborn.*

The mother had given birth to twins in a jail cell, not even making it to the infirmary. One twin was born severely deformed, and had no chance of survival. The other twin was here, still hanging on by a thread. The mother had no interest in a chaplain visit, so I stayed with the newborn in the NICU, praying while the doctors did their best to save her.

The mother didn't want to see a chaplain, that is, until she realized that, as a prisoner, the chaplain was the only person she could speak with at the hospital besides her doctor. That's better than nothing, right? As a chaplain, it was my job to serve and to comfort, without judgment of mothers handcuffed to their birthing beds, because we are all children of God.

But when I opened the door, my heart skipped a beat. I knew the woman in that bed. It was Anber's biological mother. I had been holding the baby we had been praying for since last fall. *That was Anber's baby sister.*

I couldn't be the mother's chaplain, of course, because of the boundaries and dual relationships involved, so I called for another chaplain to replace me. Our foster care resource worker had told us that since the child was going to be placed in our home, we had permission to visit her. The hospital social worker disagreed, since they didn't yet have copies of the official placement papers. Ultimately, the infant was transported to another hospital while we were still battling paperwork confusion.

I watched the helicopter take off later that morning, knowing its precious cargo was headed to the children's hospital in Oklahoma City. My arms ached to hold her, and I learned that I still had tears left after all I had already been through. I felt my mother there that day, that day I became a mother in a new way, that day I became that baby's mother somehow, when our eyes had locked and I saw life in there. I learned that day how such a little life could feel so big, how such a tiny body could be filled with such a powerful spirit, how one miracle could change the world.

I watched the helicopter cross the sky, and held my gaze upon it as it slipped past the horizon. It felt like forever before I saw her again.

Because there were drugs in her meconium, the baby was immediately placed in state custody — although, in reality, she would remain in the hospital for months. We followed every channel we could think of to get her placement papers completed, even though we knew she couldn't come home yet. Our resource worker entered our information into the computer system in bold letters for the baby's caseworker to see. Both the county where we lived and the county where Anber had been picked up considered us a kinship placement because we had already adopted Anber. Tulsa County did not agree.

The baby's first caseworker had the role of investigator, and she was focused on getting lab results and other information from the hospital in Oklahoma City. Once there was sufficient evidence for the newborn to officially be taken into custody, the case was transferred to another caseworker, who then had to search for any biological family who might want her.

We waited and waited. They told us to prepare for the baby to come home with us from the hospital after she stabilized, but also to be aware that a qualified family member could take her at any time. Some of her extended family was ruled out because of past felonies. A grandfather was willing and qualified, but then changed his mind because of his work schedule and her medical needs. The biological father's family declined any possibility of placement, due to religious reasons, stating that there was no baby because their son was not married — despite DNA results confirming him as the father. Even if all biological family was ruled out, however, we were told not to expect actual placement because no one believed the baby would live that long.

I was in the hospital, myself, for cancer drama and pneumonia, when they finally called to say that, yes, the baby was going to be placed with us. They were very explicit and careful to warn us, though, that she was considered separate from Anber's case, and would only be in our home for fostering. There were no plans at that time for adoption. The mother was going to work through the treatment plan as assigned by the court, including getting into a rehab program where mothers can have their children with them.

In the time between that call and when we first brought her home, we had a lot of confusion about the baby's progress. The doctors would report to her biological mother, or the caseworker, but not all of them talked to us. They were not trying to be cruel, but in today's world of privileged information and limited time to communicate with families, it's tricky for them to know what they can say to whom. We had cared for this baby since she was born, but were still "only" foster parents.

Foster parents get a bad reputation, I think. There are some foster parents who are terrible, just like some biological parents are terrible. There are some foster parents who foster for the wrong reason, or who neglect or harm the children worse than they were abused before coming into care. There are some foster parents who are in it for the money, which takes an extreme level of neglect, because there is not that much money provided, and certainly not enough to actually meet all of the child's needs. It was sometimes hard to find other foster parent friends who were not burned out or just crazy.

But for the most part, foster parents are really amazing people who do critical but grueling work. We open our homes not because we are perfect, but because it is the right thing to do. We share our lives not because we have so much to offer, but because those children don't have anything. We invite strangers into our families not because our families are so good, but because little ones need somewhere to belong.

The currency of foster care, as if in payment for our effort, is paperwork. There is paperwork to travel away from home for a weekend, and fingerprints to have family stay overnight. There are forms to fill out to get permission to fill out the forms to enroll other people's children in school. There are documents to show doctors that you have permission to get the child fed, bathed, dressed, and transported to their appointment, but not permission to decide what happens at that appointment. Most important are the papers that keep your home open so that more children keep coming, and the papers which tell you which children stay.

This time the paperwork helped to tip the balance in our favor. Once we were an officially documented placement family for the baby, we were finally able to talk to the hospital directly about her. She was now four weeks old, and we hadn't heard anything about her directly since the day she was born.

We learned that she had already undergone nineteen surgeries. They had created a jaw, and tried to build her a chin, but were unsure whether she would have any teeth. They had transplanted a tongue, and had sewn the tip of it to her lower lip in effort to keep her airway open. She was still on a nasogastric (NG) feeding tube and oxygen, and we would need special training classes to be able to care for her at home.

Even after all those surgeries, she still had a small jaw, recessed chin, cleft palate, and some heart problems.

Those are all symptomatic of Pierre Robin Sequence (PRS). It's called a sequence because of the order of failed development during the first eight to twelve weeks in utero. First the jaw is either stuck or does not develop. Then the tongue does not descend out of the nasal cavity, which causes the cleft palate. This even impacts the baby in utero, as the baby cannot breathe and swallow amniotic fluid normally.

With some variation, there are standard procedures about the ages in which repairs are done as the child grows up. A cleft lip is usually fixed pretty early, but the palate is often not repaired until closer to the first birthday. Interventions to help the baby's narrow airway vary, and recent research is changing how some of this is done.

PRS was the diagnosis she was given, even though she did not have any of the genetic markers that can cause it, or any of the related syndromes that sometimes co-occur. Hers was determined to have been caused by drug exposure in utero, but she would follow the same time line of surgical repairs. Regardless, like other PRS babies, her biggest challenges were her airway and feeding.

Breathing can be impacted in three ways. An obstruction in the upper airway, like a large tongue base or malformed epiglottis, can cut off oxygen. Second, these obstructions also cause carbon dioxide to build up. That is why bypassing severe obstructions, with a tracheostomy for example, is so important. Third, is that these little ones expend a huge amount of calories trying to breathe; if their airway remains compromised, they will grow slowly, if at all, even with a feeding tube providing more than the appropriate caloric intake.

Feeding must be done very carefully to prevent breathing liquids into the airway. The child may need to be fed through a tube sometimes to prevent choking. Infants with this condition should not be put on their back, to prevent the tongue from falling back into the airway.

This is why she was still in the hospital: because without a jaw, or a tongue, or the roof of your mouth, it is really hard to eat. What she did get down, would often come back up, shooting out through her nose and projecting across the room. She would gain a gram one day, and lose twenty grams the next day. She was fighting for her life, and every ounce counted.

I stayed overnight in the hospital as often as possible, learning how to feed this baby. I had to hold her on her side with her head pointed away from me, instead of on her back cradled in my arms. When eating was too stressful, she needed to be fed through a tube. Most crucial was listening for the gurgle that meant she was suffocating. I had to lay her down on her side or tummy, even though every bit of current research said to leave babies on their back. It made my brain hurt, and it made my heart hurt. But as scary as all of that was, we were eager to bring her home.

In the meantime, I was working weekends in the ER, finishing my chaplaincy training, fighting pneumonia, and dealing with cancer... plus Mary was having cochlear implant surgery, we found out we were adopting her plus the two new boys, and still had three fosters in the home. It was insane. The baby was three hours away in the hospital, and it all became a blur, like the blur of a newborn anyway, but with all those extra layers.

I had spent two busy years of children coming and going, keeping things hectic enough and loud enough to drown out my grief, but now I was taking on a living reminder of all we had lost. It was an emotional trigger for me, this risk of a baby who could die. The shadow was hidden beneath the laughter in my house full of children — that far-away, familiar feeling of having babies who don't grow, babies who die, babies who only linger as ghosts. Just as the raw trauma of my mother's death had to be faced head on and healed, I now had to face the grief of the babies I had fought for and lost, and separate it from this one who was mine but wasn't, who wasn't growing but was surviving. It was all a tangle, painful because it was still healing. I couldn't avoid it or distract from it anymore.

After fifty-one days in the NICU, it was time for the baby to discharge. We had further delays when she failed her car seat test. She could not breathe well enough to sit up even for five minutes, and we had a three-hour drive home. We had to buy a special car seat bed that let her lie flat on her stomach, with straps going over her shoulders and buckling behind her back. They warned me to keep a close eye on her for any color changes, and to stop every thirty minutes to reposition her. They sent us home without any monitoring equipment even for the drive.

I tried buckling the bed into the middle seat so that I could watch her in my rear view mirror as I drove, wondering how safe that made either of us. There was nowhere on the interstate to pull over every thirty minutes to get her out as instructed, and by the halfway point she was wailing for the food she couldn't keep down. She had pulled out her own NG tube before we left the hospital, and the nurse had not replaced it. I had no other way to get formula to stay down besides bottle feeding — which was not working. By the time we made it home, I felt a million miles away from any help and completely incompetent in knowing how to keep her alive. As I carried her car seat bed inside the house, I could feel it vibrate as she tried to breathe, stretching into the most contorted positions trying to get air.

Feeding her at home, with no emergency staff on backup, was both frightening and exhausting. We used specialty bottles, with a unique valve in the nipple, since her cleft palate meant she had no suction. She got milk out of her bottle by chewing on it, which would squirt the milk to the back of her throat. She often choked, no matter how how small the nipple we used. Nathan and I had to drape adult size bath towels over us since so much formula leaked from her mouth and shot out her nose. It would take a half-hour at a time to feed her, and she was still not keeping enough down, and she was still using all her calories to breathe. Her hands and feet and lips would turn blue and purple, and nothing we tried seemed to help.

She was precious, though, that baby I had prayed for through each arrest update, from court hearing to court hearing. I could not believe she was finally here, and alive, and doing as well as she was. Those first four weeks were touch and go, and the doctors were not sure she would live at all. But, each night was a miracle, and each morning a tiny glimmer of hope. Her eyes got brighter and brighter, and I knew she was in there, and I knew she had Anber's fighting spirit. It was an honor to hold such a being in my arms.

Our nurse practitioner did a lot of research and taught us a great deal about PRS, and we studied all we could find out about it on our own. Much of the research, as well as the parent groups online, discussed the benefits of a tracheostomy, or "trach" (pronounced *trake*), which would bypass the narrow airway by way of a small tube inserted through a hole at the bottom of the throat. For PRS children, these are often temporary and can be removed as the child grows and the airway opens.

No one wants their baby to get a trach, ever, unless their baby is purple. Then it is a Godsend. It is invasive, and it is risky, and it requires more hospitalization and surgery. Part of the hospitalization is parent training for how to clean and change the trach tube, as well as maintenance care such as suctioning mucous and secretions out of the trach to keep the created airway clear. At times, it could even require a separate room for the baby and a night nurse.

One concern some of our doctors had was that they were not sure the baby would actually be living with us. She was still a foster baby then, and her mother had every chance of getting her back. It was one thing for us to research and complete trach care training. It was another thing to send a high risk baby home to parents who may or may not be willing to complete training, remain clean and sober to manage a high risk airway, or follow up with outpatient clinics as needed. At that time, it was in her best interest not to trach her if they could care for her without it at all, just in case she got sent home unexpectedly.

Newer research also discussed mandible (lower jaw) distraction, a brutal procedure where a set of metal bars is inserted through the upper and lower jaws, and attached on each side of the face with screws, like an instrument of torture. These screws are turned several times a day, essentially breaking the jaw each time to move it out and forward, with the bones' natural healing process working overtime to lengthen it. This also brings the over-sized tongue base forward, opening the upper airway to help her breathe.

We were told that the distraction process is so intense that it's not even done in some countries, and the hospitals in our state would not do it without also doing a trach. In Britain, they usually manage the airway with a naso-pharyngeal tube, which runs from the nose down through the trachea in order to provide unobstructed breathing. If that does not create a sufficient airway, then they move to a trach. They will not do jaw surgery except as last resort, and even then, not until a child is school aged, considering America's rush to do surgery on infants to be barbaric. Some research hospitals in the United States are very aggressive, doing distractions immediately while trying to avoid a trach all together. Cincinnati Children's was one of those hospitals.

While our nurse practitioner worked on the medical side of sending referrals so the baby could be admitted in Ohio, I worked with the caseworker on getting permission from the judge and biological mother to travel. This included fighting the state's Medicaid for foster babies, where getting coverage approved for an out of state provider was an impossible feat. While they bickered about provider contracts, we had a blue baby who wasn't keeping formula down and was dipping below her birth weight. Instead of just waiting for permission, I searched online for the contact information of the ENT doctor at Cincinnati and emailed him directly to tell him about the baby.

I squealed with delight when they accepted her for a referral and agreed to consult on her case. They told me they could either bring her up to be examined there, or they could just talk to our doctor locally for consultation, if that helped. But at least she finally had the specialists she needed, and we were no longer alone. We also finally got home health set up for weekly weight checks and ear checks, with the pediatrician teaching us that her constant ear infections were due to the cleft palate. We were still fighting for pulse-ox monitors to keep a watch on her oxygen levels, and to alert us to when she stopped breathing all together. Her bassinet remained in our room, and Nathan and I took sleepless shifts for those weeks, trying to keep her alive.

During this time, we returned to Oklahoma City for an appointment at the cleft palate clinic that had been scheduled when she was first discharged from the NICU. They were concerned about how much weight she had lost, and how badly her airway was obstructing. The plastic surgeon told us that he wanted to admit her for a trach and a distraction, that she was not safe to go home, and that she should not have been discharged. However, we had to consult with the ENT first, he said, because it would be the ENT who would actually perform the surgery. But, for reasons we could not understand, the ENT didn't take her condition seriously at all. He said she was *fine* and just needed to eat more calories, even though her oxygen was in the low 70's, and he made jokes about the obstructing sounds as she breathed.

He sent us home, and I was furious. I knew she was not fine, that her color had changed drastically since being discharged from the NICU, and that she wasn't keeping any formula down. I knew she was choking and gasping, and not even sleeping well because she woke every time she stopped breathing. I felt helpless. We debated what to do, and advised the caseworker, but ultimately had to follow the plan the biological parents chose and what Medicaid approved.

Cincinnati contacted us to check on the baby's status. Explaining everything that had happened was a run-on sentence that left us out of breath. The nurse on the call was appalled, and couldn't believe that we still didn't even have oxygen monitors, or any supplemental oxygen, and told us she would consult with her team and call us back.

We were in the middle of helping the other children through homework and physical therapies when she called back. Nathan answered the phone and put it on speaker to interpret for me. "I don't want to alarm you," she said, "but you have twelve hours to get that baby here."

It turns out that, when you don't trach a baby like everyone says you should, or give her oxygen, or monitor her oxygen and heart rate and carbon dioxide, and instead just let her aspirate while trying so hard to eat and breathe, then you end up with a very sick baby who now also has cardiopulmonary hypertension. "She could die," she said, "I want you to pack a bag right now and leave for the emergency room immediately."

She told us that she had already spoken to the closest children's ER, which was still forty-five minutes away from us, and said that if they didn't have to trach her right away, and were able to stabilize her with oxygen enough to travel, then we would be put on a Life Flight immediately. *You need to be at that ER in an hour. They know you are coming.*

Nathan and I just looked at each other. Our marriage has never been, it seems, about finishing a day the way we started it, and nothing has been easy. We went into disaster drill mode: one foster child went to respite care with another foster parent, two went to extended family safe enough to keep them for the weekend, one went to a grandparent's home for the day, and that left Nathan with only our permanent placements, Alex and Anber, for the weekend. Of course that meant that I not only had to pack for the baby and myself, but also for three other children not even coming with us!

I got the children ready, and the baby ready, and me ready as quickly as I could, though I had to drive back to the house twice: once to grab the baby's placement papers, without which she would get no treatment anywhere, and once for my cancer medicine. On the forty-five-minute rush to the ER, I had to pull over twice because the baby was choking so badly in her car seat bed where she lay on her belly. I called doctors and caseworkers along the way to catch them up on what was happening, and then had to make three attempts at finding the correct entrance to the hospital parking lot, but we made it.

We had spent so much time worrying over trach versus distraction, weighing risks and benefits. But in the end, we were only foster parents. By the time the baby and I were loaded onto the Life Flight, a decision had been made for us.

# 7

Besides being a thousand miles from home, the baby and I were uprooted from the only place we had known in Cincinnati. The complex airway unit had been a safe place, where all the nurses and techs knew how hard it was for her to breathe. Respiratory therapists were just outside the door. The staff was consistent, and we were comfortable with them. The other parents were friendly, visiting in the hallway or lounge area. The day nurses knew which toys the baby liked to play with, and the night nurses knew which recordings of Nathan's violin she preferred. The techs knew how to position her just right, which blankets were the softest, and taught me how to order my food to the room so I could eat while she was sleeping. It was a warm place, and the people there felt like family.

PICU was cold and isolated. The staff there was, by necessity, focused on patients in immediate crisis rather than making families comfortable long-term. The other parents and I rarely left our rooms, all of us glued to the blinking monitors whose beeps told us our child was still alive. No food was allowed, only thin blankets were offered, and babies in comas didn't get any toys. Keeping her heart rate down was priority, so I couldn't play hymns or FaceTime with Nathan and the children, as any stimulation sent it skyrocketing. I was alone there, famished, and exhausted.

The tiny, brown and pink polka--dot dress I had brought for her to wear on Sundays lay cast aside on a counter as she lay there in only a diaper. IVs surrounded her head as they entered a central port, giving the nurses direct access rather than having to poke her so many times. Another set of IVs poked out of one of her hands. A yellow NG tube was taped across one cheek, one end heading down her nose to her stomach and the other end left hanging off the side of the bed where it was dropped after her last feeding. The distractor bars framed the sides of her face, each one capped with a rubber tip that rested on her bandage-covered chest. White straps held down her arms so that she could not pull the ventilator tubes out of her throat and nose if she woke, but she spent two weeks not waking.

I put on a black skirt and button up shirt to remind myself of the holy Sabbath, even though I would attend no service. Mortality weighted the air around me, and I needed the ritual to give me breath and nourish my spirit. I had tried all week to get in touch with a local ward (as our congregations are called due to being organized geographically) so that I could partake of the Lord's Supper and so the baby could receive a priesthood blessing. Friends back home connected me with a Mormon doctor who worked at the hospital. He was a faithful priesthood holder, and was willing to come minister to the baby and me.

There was hope in that, and comfort, and strength.

Everything would be okay then, I knew, not because of circumstances being easy, but because of a God who knows us, a Father who loves us. We were not forgotten, even so far away from home, from my work that was supposed to be paying our bills, from the air we couldn't get into her lungs. It seemed an easy thing to remember the bread and water, that Sacrament that refreshed us and renewed our covenants, and why we take it on the Sabbath.

To prepare for receiving the Sacrament, I made sure our rooms were extra clean. I washed her gently with a warm cloth, followed by lotion for her skin. I was wearing the nicest clothes that I had there, which was the chaplain outfit I had been wearing for an overnight hospital shift when we were Life Flighted to Ohio. I put us in order as best I could. I fasted instead of buying food, and whispered my scripture study to the baby. I even shared my testimony with her, as a previous priesthood blessing had instructed, promising that she would know and understand and feel it, and that it would give her strength and lift her spirits.

*I know that our Father-in-Heaven is real, and that He knows us, and that He loves us.*

*I know that we lived with Him before we came to Earth, in the same strong spirits we still are, but that we agreed to come here to get our bodies and practice making choices.*

*I know that we were trained and prepared, even set apart, for these experiences before we were born – even this one we are now enduring.*

*I know He will help us to accomplish everything He asks us to do.*

*I know that the priesthood has been restored to the Earth, and that our temples are sacred places where we can do ordinances that seal families together forever. I know that part of your purpose and my purpose is to be sealed together in the temple, and that part of that responsibility is doing ordinance work for lines of your ancestors that would not otherwise be found and rescued.*

*I know that my parents are alive in spirit, and will someday be resurrected, but because of the priesthood and because of temple blessings, we do not have to wait until then to know them or receive their help or grow our relationship with them.*

*I know that people are praying for you, and fasting for you, and that these prayers are being heard and answered.*

Just as I finished whispering to her, a nurse notified me that we had visitors. It had taken them some time to get permission to see us, she said, because the baby had no consents for visitors, and as the foster parent I was not authorized to approve any. But she laughed as she told me that the caseworker had told her I was a grownup and could have whatever visitors I wanted.

Two men from the local ward entered softly, ready to give the baby a blessing and to bless the bread and water for me, with such quiet and meek spirits that the Savior himself could have been standing before me. They anointed the baby's head with a tiny drop of oil, placing their strong hands so gently over it, and then they prayed to ask Heavenly Father for help with her healing. Finishing with words of promise from Him to her, they stepped away from the hospital bed and turned to me.

I was crying, and one of them handed a white handkerchief to me. The other silently pulled out a small cup and piece of bread, preparing the sacrament for me on a paper plate. The bread and water were blessed and passed to me, and I took them as a gift from the same God I knew back home. I soaked in the moment, with my eyes still closed and arms still folded.

Suddenly, I was jolted back to the present when the older man of the two kissed me right on my forehead!

"That's from your husband," he said.

I snorted, and began to laugh. It was so unexpected, and so out of character, and yet so perfect and right and exactly what I needed. It was like the wizard at our engagement breakfast in New York, this man appearing from nowhere to deliver a blessing from Nathan.


My mom was concerned when I was suddenly all stirred up about some Mormon boy in New York, of all places. I am sure she thought I was going to run away again. I am sure she pictured me abandoning her again in a new place away from her friends. I am sure she was wary of this stranger who was wooing her daughter — as well she should have been. If someone told me a story about meeting some guy online, and going to meet him at a random park in real life, and getting engaged the next week, I would have said they were crazy!

Except there was more to it than that. His parents were life-long members in the LDS church, so I had lots of people to verify (i.e., gossip about) who they were, and what they were like. His cousin who put us in contact certainly seemed to think highly of him. But I think, in the end, I was seduced by his writing: day after day of emailed epistles, poetry or politics, private revelations, and pure romance. No fraud could counterfeit such a high volume of consistently swoon-worthy content.

The first time we ever spoke on the phone, I had a literal confession to make. I was adamant that our friendship could not progress until I told him about my past. It was important to me, if I was going to take this relationship-possibility seriously, that he would be able to hold all the pieces of me gently, without spilling me. I needed to know that I would be safe with him before I got any further. It was only fair to this good Mormon boy to know about my life before my conversion. It was terrifying, but had to be done.

The *Reader's Digest* version of those sins? I ran away at seventeen. I lived with a family and took care of their children in exchange for a room to sleep in while I finished school. Working my way through college was about the only right decision I made, but it also introduced me to bad people who claimed to be looking out for my best interest, and good people who had standards very different from what I grew up with or would later come to adopt as my own. I learned to drink, and curse, and picked up all kinds of behaviors that I had to eliminate once I chose to be baptized. Everywhere I went, everything I did or said, seemed to cause damage to my family. I embarrassed my brother, humiliated my father, and broke my mother's heart.

It wasn't all bad, though. For a time, I went to live in the back hills of the Ozark Mountains. I learned how to build simple but elegant houses, how to dig wells, how to kayak, how to clear a field, how to keep bees, how to live in the woods, how to draw, how to paint, how to eat off the land I nurtured, how to make or consciously purchase my clothes so that women and children in other countries would not suffer because of my choices. I learned how to sing, and how to write poems, and how to breathe fresh air. I learned how to set myself free, how to dance, how to grow things in the Earth, and how to grow me. Eventually, I did some long-term therapy work on my own healing, but living so close to nature those years healed me as much as anything.

I grew up moving several times a year, and internalized the ability to just cut off and go without recognizing the damage it can cause or the need for something lasting or more nurturing. This became part of my path of destruction, running away over and over again, just as I had run away from my family. Running left me out of breath, but I kept repeating the same mistakes and making things worse each time, when I meant to make them better.

Know what Nathan said, when I told him all that — plus the details of these worst moments, and deepest shames, and darkest secrets? "It's a good thing we have the atonement. That's what it's there for, and I have really needed it, too. It's amazing how you have honored the gift of the atonement by becoming the woman that you are." I had revealed the worst parts of me, and that's what he said, without missing a beat. And I cried. And I knew, right then, that day, I would marry him.

Our wedding weekend was a year after my father had died. He had endured cancer, of an ugly sort, and spent months and months in the hospital dying. It was awful and sad. Those were exhausting days that turned into exhausting months, trying to work and drive back and forth two hours to be near the hospital. I had told my father about my conversion in those Sabbath Day letters before he got sick, and about getting baptized into The Church of Jesus Christ of Latter-day Saints. We spoke of the atonement in our few conversations during these months, recalling when I had grown up in the first pew of small, rural churches where he was the music minister. Some of my favorite childhood memories are of him leading the music for those congregations, and the dusty, dirt roads driving there and home again. My parents had taught me about the Bible, and wanted me to know those truths.

I knew God had always used prophets. If He had used prophets then, it made sense to me that He still used prophets. That was a scary thought to me at the time, because I knew the revelatory warnings about false prophets leading people into danger or even condemnation. I could not risk my soul on fallacy, but I also knew that a true prophet would testify of the Savior. A true prophet would not oppress me or tell me what to do, but rather would guide me and teach me godly principles. I would be taught to ask for myself, study for myself, and know for myself. If God still called prophets, just like in the Old Testament, then God would call the kind of prophets He has always called: the simple, the humble, the grateful. He called those who struggled to speak, so they would speak His words. He called those willing to serve, so that they would do what He asked. He called those brave enough to ask bold questions, humble enough to pray, and crazy enough to pull off miraculous works of God.

Ultimately, it was this kind of thinking that led me to getting baptized. I knew I loved my Father-in-Heaven, and had always prayed, even through my worst messes in life. I grew up with many truths taught me about God and Jesus and the disciples of old, and my skin tingled with lightning power when I first realized that this had all been restored in these last days. It was not just learning something new, or drinking the Kool-Aid. It was a remembering. It was something deep inside me that I somehow already knew was true.

Even though they initially were not thrilled with my choice of churches, both my father and mother were grateful to the Mormons for cleaning up my life and returning me to my family. While they did not agree with all its teachings, they appreciated that I was sober and trying to make amends with my family. I could not undo all I had done, and it would take a great deal of time for my family to trust me again, but the church had brought me home when nothing else had.

My father's final counsel before he passed was a warning to be careful and not let my mother take all my money, and then he added that I needed to find a husband. I took my father's counsel to heart. I am sad that he passed just months before I met Nathan. I think they would have loved each other, and have witnessed moments of their friendship growing even through the veil.

Nathan's first meeting with my mother was perfect. After one of the dates during our marathon week when Nathan was visiting me in Oklahoma, we pulled into the driveway and he politely stated, "Um, we forgot to stop at Sonic for your mom." Every day she would order cherry vanilla Diet Dr. Pepper (no ice). She was such a frequent customer that when she died, Sonic provided cups for the funeral lunch. That day, when Nathan needed to woo my mother as much as me, we left the house and then came home again with mom's usual in hand, and she was delighted. That's when I knew he would do just fine, because he knew her rules.

It was so good watching them get to know one another, to feel the love in the home, to experience the joy of doing it well, and the peace of choosing wisely. We had fun giving Nathan the tour of the house and garden and dogs. Nathan helped me clean the vegetables I picked from the garden, and then sat at the table chatting with my mom for ages. I stayed in the kitchen, watching and listening and trying not to cry. It was beautiful. I felt so full of love for them both, so in awe of the miracle, so at peace with being at-one.

My mother challenged Nathan to a round of *Take Two*, a game played with *Scrabble* tiles. I had dreaded this, and knew what was coming. Those two word-lovers were neck and neck, until the very end when Nathan was about to win. At the last moment, my mother pulled extra tiles and laid down a different word to beat him.

"That's cheating!" Nathan exclaimed.

"No. That's winning!" my mother said, as she scooped up the tiles so no one could protest.

He handled that very gracefully, despite the blatant wrong-doing, and it set a precedent. He became a stabilizing force in the relationship between me and my mother. Because he had no baggage in his relationship with her, he was able to hold his own without triggering her. He could challenge her without setting her off, and I had never in my life seen her laugh so much. Nathan was the reason my mother and I ended well, like a mediator that helped us negotiate happiness.

That's what the atonement does. Nathan spoke of it in the eulogy he gave for her only three months later: "She was a complicated woman... She was serious-minded, but also had a dry sense of humor and a quick wit. She was strong enough to survive all manner of tragedies in her life, and yet in many ways was quite fragile, and she built up a lot of defenses in order to feel safe... I think that Mom was hungry to love, and hungry to be loved, but sometimes that was hardest to do with the people she wanted to be closest to. My wife Emily likes to use the words 'in bounds' and 'in order' to describe things in the state in which they are in harmony with God's law and the principles of eternal truth. And while family 'out of order' brought her much sorrow through seasons of her life, it was family 'within the bounds' that always, always brought her the most joy.

"There were times when her family was shaken and scattered, shifting away from God's order through both choice and circumstance, but in the last few years, through the grace of Jesus Christ and by faith on His Atonement, they have been restored and made whole once more. On those Sundays when the whole family was in town and attending church together, Mom would look across at us all, taking up an entire pew, and she'd be so proud she'd nearly burst."

The Christmas before she died, the first Christmas Nathan and I shared together just two months after we were married, we got together at my mother's house with my brother's family to celebrate, and open presents, and eat and play games, and generally make a mess and lots of noise. When it was time to leave, Nathan was the last to say goodbye. My mom was watching the crowd siphon out through the front door, and her eyes filled with tears, and she said, "This was the Christmas I have always dreamed of. It was perfect." She said she had spent a lot of Christmases alone, but how she had longed to see her children together and happily married, her grandchildren, and a house full of happy chaos. She tenderly hugged Nathan goodbye, as if she had not just cheated at *Trivial Pursuit*.

She was killed only two weeks later. The night after the funeral was particularly hard for me, and I felt the old tug to just run away. I drove over to my mom's house without Nathan, parking in her garage. We had the same kind of car, and so with the garage door closed where no one could see me, I scooted down into the floorboard beneath the steering wheel, and laid my head back on the seat. It was horrifying to act out how she had died, but it was as close to her as I could get, and I sat there for a long time weeping.

When I began to be concerned for my own sanity, I wriggled back up in the seat and got out. I walked into her kitchen and across the living room toward her bedroom. Her four poster bed remained in the middle of her room, on its last night before the movers would come in the morning. I climbed up on to her bed, and buried my face in her pillow. I could still smell her, and I began to cry again.

My heart hurt so much. I hurt for the loss of her, for our hard years, and for the miscarriages. I hurt for the father I had lost, and the good friends we had been when I was young. I hurt for being alone in the world, and for not being sure anyone would ever love me the way she had.

The thought came: *run away. Go to the airport and just get on a plane. Any plane.* I considered that I could buy some alcohol and no one would know. How could they blame me? Or I could smoke, and no one would care. It was maybe the strongest I had been tempted since getting baptized, and there was a visceral pain to it.

I did not do it, not any of it. Instead, I chose trust. I called Nathan, and told him that I did not have any words, but that I could not come home yet... but also that I wanted him with me. He drove over immediately. I opened the door to let him in, and fell sobbing into his arms. The start of new whiskers scratched gently on my face. The understanding that I was an orphan washed over me, and he fell with me onto my mother's bed, just letting me cry.

There was nothing I could do to fix this. My parents were gone, and our mortal time together was over. When my father had just gone into the hospital for his cancer, my mom found out she needed emergency back surgery or she would be paralyzed. I was driven to be there for them both. I invited my mom to come live with me, even while I was commuting two hours each way to be with my father. I was fueled by a hunger for restoration, a longing to fix the family I was convinced I had destroyed, and perhaps a splash of self-punishment.

My mother had a stroke in surgery on the same day my father died, and so I had to leave her in ICU just to drive to my father's funeral. Because of our past, and because I had been gone, I did not feel very comfortable at the funeral. It was my own doing, I knew, and I didn't want to cause problems for anyone else there. I just waited until everyone left the graveside, and then went back to the grave by myself and sat down in the grass and watched them cover the grave. I stayed until the bulldozer drove away. Then I fell down on the freshly turned dirt, and cried for a really long time.

Those were hard days, but they were days that made me strong enough to be softened. I had dreamed of a restoration with my father, but the restoration that happened was the restoration of me to my true self. I had learned to stay and do my duty, giving all there was to give, without running away.

It was during these dark hours that I learned that my original running away was very much like Eve biting the apple: not okay, but kind of necessary. If I had stayed, I would have drowned trying to rescue my mother from cancer, and not finished school. If I had remained so self-righteous as in my youth, I never would have been open to embrace a fullness of truth that gave the power and authority to what I already knew was true. I don't mean that all my behavior while I was away from my family was okay, but I learned that God didn't give up on me then, even when it seemed everyone else had. I left my family because I had thought I had failed at saving them, but by grace had found the only thing that could save us. He had used what seemed like the worst part of me for good, and that was restoration. Even me, the Black Sheep, could not only be rescued, but used for good.

It reminded me of the painting I always see in the waiting room at the LDS temple in Oklahoma City. It's the Minerva Teichert one that makes me think of me, that black sheep — not just because it's a black sheep, but because it is a lamb. It took me a long time — until I saw my brother's children, actually — for me to realize that I had only been a child, only a lamb, when all of the chaos started. I had been so young! *Only a lamb!* Not that it excuses anything, but understanding that was an opening for me to start learning to find mercy for myself.

That's when I met Nathan. Only a few months had passed after burying my father. My mother was home from the hospital, recovering, and still living in my home. I had been to Israel and back again for the first time. I threw stones in the water there in Galilee, letting go of my sins and shadows and grief, and brought a few small stones back to hide in the Earth around my father's grave. I continued fervently studying about the temple, and still went several times a week. This was the end of a season, finally, but also the beginning of something I did not yet understand.

In some ways, my father's passing made the beginning of this new time in my life feel especially sacred. At times, it felt like I had access to him like never before, without interference. Whenever I testified of my new faith, I shared it with him. When I gave a talk in church, I thanked him for coming. When I felt his presence at the temple, or in other sacred moments, I greeted him warmly and confidently, with tears and a tender heart in awe at what the Savior's promise has done for all of us. When I made a good choice, I did so knowing he would see the difference between who he had thought I was and who God was helping me become. It changed everything, and in these ways, I tried, finally, to honor him. I found peace — not just with him, but with myself.

# 8

Standing next to the cold rails of the hospital bed on that hot summer day, with cold air blowing on my head and arms, and my feet tangled in cords and tubing from monitors and tanks all around me, I stared at my too-small three-month-old daughter lying in a full size hospital bed. It was elevated, and she was spread out on an incline, her legs and wrists in tiny restraints clipped to the bed sheet. Vials and IVs poked out of one arm, covered with a tiny guard covered in tape, giving her the appearance of being prepared for a hockey game as much as the fight of her life. Wires from oxygen and heart rate monitors covered her feet and chest. The white and blue intubation tubes came out of her nose, hissing to the sound of the ventilator that kept her alive, with a hospital gown covering her but not really attached to her.

I had awakened early, forcing my body out of the thin blanket and off of the hard recliner to shower before rounds happened at six a.m. The early morning and the cold room left me shivering, but the doctors always spoke to me differently when I was clean and dressed up in work clothes. This was a tip given to me by another mother of a medically fragile child, and though my body was exhausted and uncomfortable, I had found it was true: the doctors took more time, looked at me more directly, and gave me more information when I was dressed professionally than when I was dressed like a mom.

We had prayed so hard for her for so long. Counting the time from when we first found out about the pregnancy in court, and including the time she spent in the hospital after she was born, we had prayed for her for a year before we were able to actually hold her. That's why, in the stupor of grief and exhaustion, on particularly long nights in the hospital watching her on life support, I worried that this was our fault, too, that maybe we shouldn't have prayed so hard for this little one to survive. What kind of life was this that she had now?

*This is not the end of your story*, I would whisper to her. *You are not alone.*

It's so hard to comfort a baby you can't pick up, when all the normal things don't work. I used to be able to make her smile by tapping her nose, but now there was a feeding tube there. I used to be able to calm her by rubbing her hair, but now it was all wrapped up in bandages. I used to be able to pat her back to help her relax, but now, because of the hardware on her face, lying on her back was the only option. She couldn't use a pacifier because her mouth was locked open. Her arms and legs were full of IVs, so I couldn't massage those, either. Finding little ways to calm her, like dolls or blankets, was one of the ongoing challenges of that hospital stay.

I waited in the hallway outside her room as she slept that early morning. I was hungry because my breakfast had arrived but so had the team of doctors, residents, and specialists. They stood in a circle outside the baby's room, with laptops on high rolling tables, discussing her progress. The big news this morning was that they would finally be bringing her out of sedation and getting her extubated. I could hold her again after that, they said, when all the tubes were out of her throat.

She was given the go ahead for extubation at 6:30 in the morning. The first step would be simple enough: bringing her out of sedation. They would have to take her off the pain medication, long enough to be sure she was alert and breathing. She would have to face the onslaught of all her pain, and I was not allowed to comfort her – not to hold her hand, brush her hair, pat her, nothing – because she had to wake up as much as possible and be breathing as strongly as she could to be able to be extubated.

She got good and mad, as she should, to be hurting that much and not given any comfort or help. As it turns out, babies breathe the best while they are crying. It's something that gave us strength in the months to come: crying is breathing. As parents of a medically fragile baby, we learned to be okay with crying, grateful even. *Crying is breathing*.

Bringing her out of sedation took about three hours. It took three hours to get her good and mad, terrified and crying, cold and hungry and wet enough to make her really cry. I cannot imagine how she felt or what she endured. I only know that I couldn't stop crying, and that my arms physically ached to hold her, to reach out to her, even just to sing to her. But I could do nothing, because they needed her to do everything. They wouldn't even let me play Nathan's violin music or sing to her. It was terrible, and there was nothing I could do to help or rescue her.

*Welcome to therapy, baby girl.* She looked at me, for the first time, with eyes that knew she had been betrayed. And I wept. Everyone cried, actually, all of us just standing around the room watching the monitors, watching her cry, waiting for her to stay awake and breathe.

There were risks to this process, they said, including congestive heart failure, heart attack, stroke, and medical cerebral palsy or other brain damage. They were also simply worried about her actual capacity to breathe. The trachea would swell after extubation, they reminded me, because of the tubes having been down her throat, and when they removed them, her airway would close up too much for them to be able to get the tubes back in. She was going to have to do this on her own, and it was going to be scary. We could only hope for the best case scenario, that she would have a simple extubation followed by strong breathing.

They called the chaplain for me before starting. I knew, in part, that her presence meant this was risky for the baby. She was prepared to either comfort me after the ordeal if she lived or console me if she died.

When it was time, they hovered over her, this mad baby, to remove stitches from inside her nose. These stitches were helping to hold the tubes for her ventilator, which had been placed at the beginning of her surgery. They had been stitched in because it was so critical that they not come out until the exact right moment.

Now I watched as this baby, no bigger than my hand, screamed in pain and wrenched in fear against the restraints. She fought the doctors as much as she could, turning her head away as they leaned over her with strangely shaped scissors. They finally got all of the stitches except for one long piece, which they left in there because she was so mad by now that she almost wasn't breathing anyway. They told me that once the tubes were free, they would just take them out and deal with the stitch later.

Then, almost without warning, the room became one of those moments where life moves in slow motion. Doctors surrounded her. One had a ventilator bag ready to breathe for her. Another had an oxygen mask ready. Residents and nurses and respiratory therapists stood by on alert. One of the doctors stepped forward, reached for the ventilator tube, and faster than I could see what was happening, pulled it out of her nose. She immediately flat-lined on every monitor. It was like Christmas lights. Suddenly every panel was flashing red.

My mind sucked me out of the room, as if I were standing very far away, watching all of this happen on a tiny screen at the end of a hallway. Everything froze, and faded, and I was suddenly confused. *Why are we here? Why is this happening? What is going on? Why are these people killing the baby they were supposed to save?*

As I stood there shivering, with the cold air blowing on me, I forced myself to move just so that I could breathe, just so that I could will her to breathe. I pulled my phone from my pocket, and started taking pictures because it was the only thing I knew how to do. Taking pictures wouldn't save her and would probably keep me in the way, but I didn't know what else to do. *She will make it through this, so don't worry. She needs these pictures for her life book, because it's part of her story. I need to be able to show Nathan, so I'm not alone in going through this.* Snap. Snap. Snap. I took pictures as they worked on her, covering her face with a tiny mask pushing oxygen and helium into her fragile lungs.

Her whole face was bright red, intensely red like a crayon, a color of red that no person's face should ever be. There was frothing of something around her mouth, and she coughed up foam, which meant her lungs were collapsing. It was a moment of horror, my skin hot under the cold air.

I wanted to make comments about what a little fighter she had always been, so that I could break the tense moment with a joke about her feisty big sister. I could maybe tell the story about the time Anber punched the daycare photographer, breaking his glasses and giving him a black eye, all because he asked her to smile. I wanted them to start talking about what a miracle baby she was, and how proud of her we all were. I wanted them to smile at the baby and talk about her adorable hair and those big eyes that suck you all the way in until you're lost. But no one said anything. I don't think anyone was breathing. They weren't even shouting directions anymore. Everyone was just staring at the monitors… until she finally gasped for breath.

Her heart rate shot up as high as 296, rising as fast as her oxygen levels plummeted. I could feel the chaplain standing behind me, and noticed when she gently rested her hand on my back. This gentle gesture simultaneously sent both comfort and fear into my veins, and caused me again to shiver with cold. I pushed past the giant canisters full of helium to get closer to the baby, squeezing between respiratory therapists and doctors to wrap my arms around her. They wouldn't let me scoop her up yet, but I wanted to comfort her, and I needed to let her know she was not alone. My arms ached to hold her after these long weeks of watching her sleep. Still, no one spoke, and tears burned my eyes.

I leaned over the hospital bed with my arm wrapped over and around her head, stroking her forehead as the only spot not covered in tubes and vials. My own tears dropped on the cotton sheet as I watched giant tears roll out of her eyes. She screamed and screamed in silence, not making a sound, because her throat was swollen and raw. Her body contorted, gasping for air that wasn't coming, and her skin changed from red to purple, and then blue, and then gray. She started retracting, gulping her stomach up into her rib cage in effort to breathe, creating a terrible wrenching sound like duct tape being pulled.

She was still heaving, still silently screaming, still desperate for air when they lifted her from the bed and gave her to me. They told me to rock her and try to calm her, a last ditch effort to help her breathe. Hot tears fell from my cheeks as her tiny body rested in my arms, after weeks of waiting for her to wake up. *Breathe, baby! Breathe!*

Out of the corner of my eye, I saw the chaplain take a step toward us.

"No!" I said, lifting a hand to hold her back. *No,* I hissed, wiping tears off my cheeks. There would be no more crying. Time was up for that, and it was time to fight.

*Breathe, baby.* I whispered to her, pleading, knowing she was trying as hard as she could.

The doctor stepped toward me, clearing his throat and nodding at the chaplain.

"NO!" I said nearly shouted. We weren't done here. We didn't fly all this way for her to die so far from home. We didn't fight through so much foster hell to lose one in the hospital. We didn't fight so hard to get here just to give up now. *Breathe, baby! Breathe!*

The chaplain motioned toward the door, and the room began to clear. The chaplain did not leave, but backed away from me until she was leaning against the window sill opposite us. She folded her arms around the book she was holding, and began to hum softly — to herself or to me, I wasn't sure. Maybe it was for the baby.

I don't know what song she hummed, but it slowed time and carried me away, reminding me of the early days with this sweet baby girl. I remembered how I used to hold her for hours as an infant in the hospital, with her doll-sized head on my chest. I would stroke her hair as her little body rose and fell with my own breathing, knitting us together outside the womb. The notes from the chaplain's song seemed to do this for us now, syncing us together in our breaths. I realized the calmer I became the more air the baby got, and that she really was trying to match her breath to mine. I slowed my breathing, going deeper and deeper with each inhalation and slowing down each exhalation, leading her to breathe with me.

That's when I saw her eyes flutter, and that's when I saw her look at me. She looked at me like she remembered, too. She looked at me like she knew I was her mother, that I would always be her mother, and that she chose me just as I had chosen her. I saw her choose to stay with me. *I saw her choose to live.*

There was a specific moment, one of the most powerful in my life, when I saw that little baby girl choose life.

And she took a breath.

And another, still retracting.

And another, still gulping.

In and out we breathed, together, slowly, and deeply, and more and more quietly.

Her body began to relax, her breaths came more regularly, and the color returned to her cheeks.

I didn't notice the chaplain tiptoe back over to us until she lifted a blanket from the bed onto the baby for me to wrap her in against me. "She's beautiful," she said, "and the Lord has delivered her to you."

Delivered to me. Me, who could not deliver any child alive. Me, who had lost every child, who had lost all my family, who did not deserve a child. *What mercy was this?*

The Lord had delivered a breathing child to my arms. *Lord, have mercy.*

*Breathe, baby girl,* I whispered.

Baby girl. *My* baby girl. My baby girl was breathing.

The Lord, in His mercy, had delivered to me a baby girl. That's when I knew what we would name her: *Kyrie.* Pronounced Keer-ree-ay, it is a Greek name of one of the prayers in the Catholic Mass. It means *the Lord delivers,* and specifically in the mass, it is *mercy* that is delivered. The Lord has had mercy on me, and in that mercy, delivered to me a breathing baby girl. *Kyrie,* I whispered. *We will call you Kyrie.* She blinked at me, as if she knew this already. *Kyrie. Lord, have mercy.*

I held that baby, and I rocked her, and I sang to her, and I patted her little bottom until she began to calm, until her gulps for air settled into shudders. She stopped sucking her stomach up into her chest with each inhalation, and she no longer sounded like duct tape being ripped off the roll. She was still the wrong color, and gurgled with each breath, but tears stopped falling from behind the oxygen mask that was too big for her face.

There was something powerful about being able to hold her, about being able to touch her, about being able to brush the dark hair out of her eyes. After weeks of waiting for her to wake up, there was something profound in the relief of being able to do something, anything, even if all I had to give were kisses all over that cherub face. I knew she wasn't safe yet, and that we were still in the middle of the hardest part, but she was trying.

Because her heart rate was dangerously high, Kyrie was sedated again. Her carbon dioxide levels were also nearly as high as her oxygen was low. A nurse listened to her chest, and explained that the helium being delivered with her oxygen would make the air lighter and easier for her to breathe until she was better able to do it on her own. It took several more days of first weaning her off the helium, and then off the oxygen, and then working out pain management, before she was stable. They were scary days in which I did not leave her side, days in which I called Nathan on FaceTime so that he could whisper to her as she slept.

Her mandible distractors were in place, and I turned them twice a day even while she was sedated. They got two turns each time: once on one side, then twice on the other side, then a second turn on the first side. I couldn't believe how quickly her jaw was growing, and the quick results seemed a miracle. By the time the distractors were removed a month later, her jaw had moved forward three inches.

The comfort I could now give her was the holding, but also the normalizing. She would realize that I could still rock her like always, but that once I did put her down I wouldn't fret over her. She would realize I could check her NG tube or diaper like normal, without scary green gloves doing things that hurt. She would realize I could suction the fluids from her mouth without her choking and losing her airway, *because she has one now.* We learned these things together, and as the days passed, she began to sleep more and more, settling into her natural routine.

Finally, another week later, for the first time since before surgery, I fed her in my arms, she fell asleep rocking, and stayed asleep when I laid her down (with a prayer). To me, it was a miracle. To me, she was a miracle. To me, we were a miracle. Because even in those really hard moments, I remembered how long I had prayed for her and wanted her and loved her. I remembered how long I had known her. Sometimes miracles are big ones, but sometimes little things are miracles, too. Such miracles and mercies could be found, even in the middle of sorrows and sufferings.

# 9

It was the day after Kyrie woke up from the coma that Ronald McDonald House of Cincinnati (RMHC) called and offered us a room. RMHC was next door to the hospital, with recently expanded facilities to include several buildings, a playground, and a garden area. Kyrie could not yet come with me, but I could sleep and eat there, and she could join me once she was well enough to be discharged to intensive outpatient care. RMHC had a crib ready to set up for her as soon as she was released, and it was such a relief to me, and made caring for her long-term possible when we were so far from home.

Getting a room there was one of our miracles. When she coughed up her NG tube, we could walk across the street to the ER and have them put it back in for us. When she stopped breathing, we would be rushed over for an oxygen mask. The front desk accepted deliveries for us — supplies for the suctioning machine, or oxygen, or feeding tubes, or the variety of tapes to keep it all in place on her little body — even while we were over at the hospital in appointments. And anytime she slept for even a few minutes, I was able to run downstairs and eat, or lay in a soft bed and sleep, or get a shower and change into fresh clothes. We couldn't have done those hard months without that home away from home.

When it was time for Kyrie to be discharged from the hospital, it was almost like bringing home a different baby. She was almost six weeks older, starting to show expression in her face, able to roll over, and learning to crawl — all of which was complicated by the bars protruding from her jaws and the feeding tube taped to her back so it didn't dangle as she tried to move around. Now that she could breathe and was getting more calories via tube feeding, she had jumped from preemie-sized clothes to an age-appropriate three-month-old size. The concierge had to go shopping for me, and RMHC signed for me when the new pajamas and baby clothes were delivered. Unfortunately, she couldn't have shirts that pulled on over the distractors, so instead of cute outfits, I had to find Onesies I could scoot onto her from the bottom up.

It took me several trips to move all our things over to RMHC, after living in the hospital for so long. Kyrie finally passed the car seat test, showing that she could safely sit upright in a regular car seat while maintaining her oxygen levels, so the local ward found a stroller for me to borrow. I got to take her on her first walk, pushing her down the sidewalk and across the street. I was nervous, but she was very excited for the change of scenery!

Everyone, staff and other parents, celebrated when I walked in the doors of RMHC with Kyrie. They understood what a huge accomplishment it was to have made it to outpatient care, and even without entirely knowing her details, they recognized she had won a fight for her life. I was proud of her, too, and surprised her with a homemade "Welcome Home" sign hung over her crib in the little room.

There was a pretty rough adjustment period for us both — rough enough that I had to do laundry three times that first day. She coughed up her NG tube twice, and threw up all of three feedings. She was also still withdrawing from the sedation drugs, and completing her course of Methadone and Ativan left her restless and agitated. She only slept for about five minutes every hour, waking with an awful scratchy cry, her throat still raw from the tubes. I was alone in that little room, trying to keep a baby from drowning in her own fluids by using a suctioning machine at regular intervals day and night, while metal bars through her face were preventing her from being able to close her mouth or swallow.

Besides that, we were coming out of a three-week hospital stay where every whimper was answered by twenty ladies in love with her, there was staff enough to meet her every need, and she was awakened every hour for vitals and checks whether she needed it or not. That meant she no longer remembered how to sleep for a whole hour, and she would get mad if I didn't come quickly enough when she cried for me.

Without a whole staff of nurses to help me, I had plenty of work to do. Changing her NG tube bandage was terrifying, because the tapes are tricky and if I messed up by dislodging the tube while trying to tape it, then that was an automatic trip to the ER. The placement of the tube had to be confirmed by X-ray, and if it got moved (such as by a baby who didn't appreciate having a tube in her nose) it could mean pumping three ounces of formula straight into her lungs. That's bad. Hearing parents are trained to replace the tube themselves by listening for air bubbles with a stethoscope, but with my cochlear implants, there was no way for me to do that and no one who knew how to train me otherwise.

By myself, with no one to help hold her, I had to remove the top layers of tape without pulling the tube out, all while she was screaming and clawing at me. Then I had to pull off the layer of tape under the tube and against her face, still without moving the tube. Then I had to cut a new skin layer of tape, get it down on her cheek, lay the tube against it, and cover it with the tape that held it on the other tape. Then there was a third layer of tape to protect all of that, because those two layers don't much like to get wet, and Kyrie got really good at pulling them off. All this had to be done with one hand, while the other hand focused on keeping the tube at the right numbered length at her nose. When I finished, my hands would be shaking as my body pumped with adrenaline.

Mealtimes were no easier, because I had to get her feeding tube ready all by myself. What may have been only seconds felt like hours as she screamed, impatient not only for me to get her tube put together, but also for that feeling of fullness to come so that she would know she had eaten even though no bottle had touched her lips. It took me a lot of practice to be able to position her correctly, holding the tubes straight up in the air while feeding her, allowing gravity to slowly pull the formula down, rather than forcing it with a syringe. It would have been easier to just do the tube feeding while she was lying down, but holding her and cuddling her while she "ate" was so important. After four months of feeding her bottles with her body turned away from me, it was the first time I could feed her while looking into her eyes.

Time would stretch as I sat there with her in my lap, my arms raised like Moses to keep her gravity feed going. I wondered who would come and prop my arms up so that we could win this battle, which made me think of play acting Bible scenes with my brother when we were little. Then I remembered how, as a young girl, I had learned to pray for the children I would someday raise. I remembered that first year of marriage, when we had one miscarriage after another, and it felt like what I needed more than anything was to hold one baby still alive.

I remembered the faces of each of the children who had come and gone from our home, and how some never looked back, and others grieved as we did when it was time to go. I remembered how fourteen-month-old Anber had bucked against us when we tried to hold her, burped herself after the bottle she wouldn't let us touch, and how she hit and screamed instead of cooing and cuddling. I remembered our first infant, who was relocated after we had her older sister hospitalized for psychiatric issues. I remembered the first newborn we brought home from the hospital, the one they moved after my cancer diagnosis. I remembered the baby with whom I seemed to share an instant spiritual connection, who was sent to live with her loving grandparents, but who was brought back time and again for child care, and whom I know I will meet again one day. I remembered the day we found out Anber's mother was pregnant, and marveled at how in spite of everything, that baby was still in my arms. I smiled down at her now as her eyes fluttered closed, milk pouring into her belly through the yellow tube in her nose.

I thought about how we prayed so hard for Kyrie before she was born, and wept each time her mother was arrested again. I thought about how they said Kyrie wouldn't be born alive, and then told us she wouldn't live the first thirty days, and then told us she wouldn't live the first three months. I looked at her now, breathing and gaining weight with the feeding tube, and enduring her first jaw distraction. I held her close in one arm, while the other arm stayed steady over my head, both arms aching and on fire from not being able to move, and I watched her sleep. I did it, these hard things, no matter how much my arms burned, because I was her mama.

Whether or not Kyrie was breathing would be our ongoing battle, even after we made it back home to Oklahoma. She got pneumonia almost every month from aspirating, even though we were working closely with a speech-pathologist to teach her to swallow safely and mange her saliva secretions. We taught her to pace herself when drinking, swallowing only three times before pulling her bottle (and later her cup) down for a breath. We used a thickener in all her liquids, keeping a honey-like consistency to slow the pull of gravity as the liquid traveled down her throat. We were always alert to respond to choking, but there was also the risk of silent aspiration — the inhaling of her liquids and secretions without us being able to hear when it happened.

She continued to need oxygen, on and off, and the hum of the oxygen concentrator became the soundtrack of our home. Her skin offered a shifting color palate of oxygenation: healthy baby pink, dusky brown, scary blue, and sometimes purple or even black. Her desats — episodes when the monitors would alert us to a drop in the oxygen saturation in her blood — were sudden and unpredictable. Our pediatrician theorized that one reason she had such an inconsistent presentation was because of her prenatal drug exposure, resulting in erratic symptoms that didn't always follow what was expected for her official diagnosis. Her cyanosis, the blue color of her hands and feet, remained so bad that the pulmonologist told us that this was just her baseline. Our safety plan became calling for help only when her sats went below 70%.

When we had to call for an ambulance, we would be taken to the nearest children's ER, which was forty-five minutes away. Kyrie would be swabbed to check for viruses, have blood drawn for blood gas analysis, be given oxygen, and strapped to monitors. By that time, her condition might appear perfectly fine again, so that we felt crazy trying to explain what had happened. Other times she struggled to recover. Consistently, it took her about four days following these severe desats for her behavior and function to return to normal.

Doctors, nurses, and specialists of all kinds continued to tell us over the next year that she needed a trach. Even though a trach introduced new risks, it would bypass the narrow airway and provide air to her lungs — and to her brain, which we were fighting to protect. While she could more and more frequently hold her sats, her weight, activity, and development were being impacted as she conserved her energy for breathing. She was scheduled for a trach three different times, but it was canceled at the last minute because of improved sats or good numbers on a sleep study. Then the doctors would just modify her oxygen plan, or take away oxygen all together because she was "fine". When they only focused on her numbers instead of her whole development, they could not understand our urgency or concerns. She was maintaining her sats at the expense of her weight, growth, and development. We always followed our directions, but the results included weight loss, almost no growth in length, and a fussy baby begging for air and unable to stay awake. She could breathe well enough to keep her numbers in an acceptable range on the monitors, but not well enough to run and play like a toddler should.

Her care team in Oklahoma suggested removing her adenoids, tonsils, and even shaving her epiglottis, but there was nothing wrong with her adenoids or tonsils, and shaving her epiglottis seemed awfully permanent. While those are common surgeries, they can also affect speech and she was already likely to have many challenges in that area.

Cincinnati's plastic surgeons twice offered to help her with a second jaw distraction. Some PRS babies undergo multiple distractions during their lifetimes, while others have airways and jaw structures that will grow with them without any procedures. The goal of distraction was to move the tongue base forward, thus opening the upper airway, but this was not guaranteed to be effective, nor was it always sufficient for every child. We knew Kyrie would probably require more distractions in time, but hoped to put it off as long as possible.

While Kyrie's first jaw distraction absolutely saved her life, the process only opened up the very top of her airway, not the lower part which remained too constricted and the wrong shape. Unlike the plastic surgeon, however, the airway team shared our concern about doing further distractions, remembering the test results that showed how her small airway was in some ways protecting her from aspirating. Opening it up too much could cause her to aspirate more often.

Instead, we fought hard for a trach, not taking lightly the severity of such an intervention. Unlike so many other treatment options, a trach would be temporary and could be removed later as she grew. A trach would give consistent air for her brain and body to grow and develop, while giving her freedom to function and play as a toddler should. Time and again, the doctors told us it was what she needed, and then changed their minds when they saw she could hold her sats.

We found an ENT in Utah who had experience working with other PRS babies who could hold their sats but did so at the expense of their development. Unfortunately, Medicaid denied us any help in getting her there or paying for him to see her, so we held a fundraiser and paid for it ourselves with help from the community which had come to rally around this little girl that so many loved. The ENT understood her airway immediately, and we were relieved to hear him talk about keeping her safe with as little intervention as possible for as long we could, but also not risking her development when she needed support. He recommended the trach option, pointing out how obstructions in PRS babies are variable and inconsistent, even from one sleep study to the next. He also confirmed what we had seen, that just because the monitor or blood gas numbers were okay didn't mean she wasn't working too hard to breathe, function, grow, or develop.

Blue babies are never okay, he told us.

Toddlers that just lay down on the ground because they are too tired to stand are not *fine*.

A baby whose weight doesn't even scrape the lowest percentile, month after month, is not *healthy*.

We continued to beg Medicaid to contract with Primary Children's Medical Center in Utah, so that we could take her there for a trach. They continued to deny us, arguing that there was no reason to go to Utah for the procedure, even when we explained it was because no one in Oklahoma would do it. All the while, Kyrie fell further and further behind in gross motor development — culminating in her finally losing the use of her left side altogether, being diagnosed with medical cerebral palsy.

Cognitively, she was quite bright, and socially she was charming. Emotionally, she was expressive, and her fine motor skills were developed while she sat so still or even laid down resting. But the gross motor skills, like running and playing and climbing, were a struggle because she didn't have the energy she needed. Her chest cavity didn't grow because she wasn't using her lungs enough to breathe deeply, and her abdominal and back muscles were stiff, with hiked up shoulders from fighting for air every second of every day.

We thought for sure that Medicaid would see that getting Kyrie a trach would save them money, rather than repeatedly paying for hospitalizations that did nothing. Every doctor we met was surprised it hadn't already happened, but none of them were willing to actually do it. Instead, they waited and waited and waited, while our concern grew about the potential impact of spending her first year without enough oxygen. I wanted that Medicaid doctor in charge of approving (or denying) her special contracts to spend a day doing his paperwork under water, and see how well he could breathe and get things done.

These issues were compounded as we prepared for Kyrie's palate repair at ten months. Her cleft palate was so extreme that the ENT said it was basically just a cleft, with no palate at all. Kyrie had learned to breathe through the open hole in what should have been the roof of her mouth, so what would happen when it was closed? The distraction had opened up the top of her airway by moving the tongue base forward, but at palate repair, her tongue-lip adhesion would also be released, adding the risk of her tongue falling back into her throat again. We were told to expect and prepare for her to be in crisis.

Following palate repair, she would not be allowed a bottle or even a sippy cup with a tip inside her mouth, because of the risk of damaging the newly-constructed palate. She would need to be drinking from an open cup if we didn't want a feeding tube after surgery. We started when she was four months old, by just giving her a cup to play with as a toy, and at five months started holding it to her lips in pretend play. By six months, we were giving her sips of actual thickened formula out of the cup, but only after she had already eaten from her specialty valve bottles, so that she wasn't too hungry. By seven months, she was trying to help hold the cup, and drank all her formula from it except for the first and last feedings of the day. By eight months, the little genius was completely off the bottle two months early.

During the final months before surgery, we gave her stage one baby food out of the cups as well, in addition to her formula, to prepare her for more nutrients and tastes, and to help avoid food and texture aversions post-repair. By the time palate repair happened at ten months, she was ready, although she still had never had any table foods. But, she was completely weaned and able to feed herself from a cup.

In January, we prepared for another big surgery, but this time with the whole family in tow. While Nathan and I were trading off time at the hospital, new friends made themselves available to watch over our rambunctious children. The children were eager to explore all the places they had heard about me visiting with the baby last summer.

The week of palate repair started with more miracles. The judge ruled that, while Kyrie's biological parents had the right to sign surgical consents, they did not have the knowledge or experience with the baby to make health care decisions for her. If the mother failed to sign consents for recommend procedures or surgeries, she would be in contempt of court with added charges of medical neglect.

And that's exactly what happened. She was supposed to be available by phone for consents before surgery, but she had completely disappeared. The caseworker couldn't find her, and the hospital couldn't get ahold of her. The judge had to sign an actual court order for the baby to have surgery the next day.

What was scariest about surgery this time, was that we didn't know exactly which procedures would be done. The goal was palate repair, of course, but a trach was possible as well. The Cincinnati surgeons were capable of doing the trach, but philosophically opposed. It was during testing on this visit that they confirmed medical cerebral palsy, which made me angry because it could have been avoided with a trach in the beginning. They were also still considering a gastronomy tube (G tube), because, even with our intensified feeding efforts, she was still too small for her age — still not even on the growth charts. The possibility of a second jaw distraction was also still looming in the shadows, if they felt her airway was too compromised.

"Regardless," they said, "no matter what we need to do, we are fighting for her life."

Maybe that's why I was awake at 4 a.m., telling myself I was awake just because there was work to do. I crept into the children's rooms to lay out their clothes. There were socks and underwear, yellow shirts, and blue overalls: matching outfits that made them look like the little minions they were. I wanted them to know that they had everything they needed, that I thought of them, even in the middle of the night, and that pieces of our life were still the same. I marked pages for them to do in their homeschool workbooks, because that was another gift: stability.

It was a blessing to be there as a family, despite the chaos, experiencing that together and not so far apart as last time. I continue to be grateful to new friends for hosting us, and to our community for helping us get there. They had supported us through fundraisers that included a dinner theater, a violin album Nathan released on iTunes, a GoFundMe project to buy a travel concentrator, and even t-shirts that said, "Go, Baby, Go" to match a YouTube video the other children made to the tune of "Johnny B. Goode". Besides all of this help, loving church members at home and in Ohio set aside a special day of fasting and prayer for Kyrie.

We planned to wake the baby for one more feeding, but before we were up, she stopped breathing. Three minutes of her gulping and gasping and choking seemed like hours as we tried to help her. *We're so close, Baby Girl, breathe!*

Once she was stable again, she cried because it scared her, too. But again, crying is breathing, and I was relieved. Her head lay on my chest, and I sat very still, and together we took deep, slow breaths. She wouldn't be able to eat after 5:15, so we tried to feed her one last time, hoping her airway wasn't compromised. She smiled up at us, full of trust.

We showered. We dressed. We packed our toiletries, in case we didn't get to come home that night. We did our couple's scripture study, and prayed together.

Kyrie had received many priesthood blessings in her short life. They always had said she would not live long, but the one before this surgery promised she would survive the procedure. They said it would be miraculous, and that it would be possible because of the faith and fasting of those around her. Through these blessings, Heavenly Father had promised she would live long enough to be sealed in the temple. We could feel those blessings cover us now, surrounding us, and we knew they were true.

Morning finally came, and we loaded her into the van. We kissed the freshly-showered heads of children. They were skittish saying their goodbyes to Kyrie. They knew the doctors had told us this could be goodbye for the last time. But it seemed like a normal day to them, with granola for breakfast, and homework waiting, and big adventures planned. Kyrie waved goodbye to them, like she was just going to one more doctor appointment and would be home in an hour.

We arrived at the hospital on time, and kept smiles on our faces as best we could. Kyrie was hungry, and we had to keep her busy. They let us go back with her to the operating room, which was very kind. We were honest with Kyrie about what was happening, even if the anesthesiologist didn't believe that she would understand. We had time to say goodbye and give her kisses, and we reminded her of all her promises. She responded by signing "diaper", and getting one last change. Then it was time. Once again, we entrusted her to others we barely knew.

We waited for ages, hours past when we expected to know something. Finally, around 2 p.m., the pulmonologist came out with an update. He said her tongue was too far back, that her airway was too narrow near the voice box, and that her misshapen epiglottis would sometimes block it, which explains some of her sudden desats. "All of this is better than before, however," he said, "and it looks like the first jaw distraction last summer was a success." But she was still in surgery with plastics, who were working on her palate and her tongue.

A two-hour surgery became a nine-hour ordeal. The plastic surgeon finally came out to tell us that they almost lost her twice in surgery, and again at extubation. She had stitches back and forth across the length of her new palate, all the way from the back to the front of her gums. Her cleft palate had been so severe, in fact, that they expect the repair will pop a hole as she grows, and need to be fixed again. She got tubes in her ears to help with the chronic infections common to cleft palates babies. She also got stitches along both her tongue and her lip where they had been attached, and one big stitch at the tip of her tongue, tying it to her cheek until she was strong enough to keep it out of her throat by herself. It would take another six months of speech therapy for her to be able to use her tongue, and it still weaves oddly to one side when she tries.

Even with a successful surgery, the twenty-four hours that followed were hard. Kyrie stopped breathing a couple times. Whenever she tried to clear her secretions, blood poured out of her nose. Nathan held her through the night, and she slept as long as he rocked her. I took my shift at 5 a.m., playing the mean mom as I cleaned up all the blood again, made her try to eat, gave her a bath, and massaged her with lotion. I changed her clothes to a new, homemade hospital gown, given to us by a thoughtful friend, paired with polka dot leg warmers. I combed her hair and put in a new bow.

Later that day, I called for a patient advocacy meeting. That brought together most of her treatment team plus a chaplain, which made for a crowded room. I was sure that it also meant they dinged her chart with some kind of crazy-mom warning that pops up whenever we come.

I started by thanking them. This hospital, for a child with PRS, is one of the best in the world. The complex airways unit, in which we had spent so much time, had a wonderful staff and felt like family to us. They had gone above and beyond to keep our baby safe and comfortable and happy. The nurse practitioners on both the plastics and the airway teams were fantastic, attentive, and encouraging. They communicated their knowledge well, and quickly responded to all of my questions.

I shared concerns about two of the doctors: one of them was the best, and one of them was the most experienced. However, they never came on rounds, wouldn't respond to messages, and never had any contact with us except immediately after surgery. I never liked what they did while they were doing it, but they pulled it off every time. I had to acknowledge that I was glad they had been on her treatment team, and that there was no way this baby would be alive without their skill.

But I also called them daredevils. Their work was risky, but in an edgy-like-artwork kind of way. No one else in the world would even dare to do what they try, I don't think, but there's a fine line between skill and foolishness. And just because you can do something, doesn't mean you should.

I told them that it was not okay to risk my baby's brain or life for research. I told them that I was a clinician, and a researcher, and a nerd of all sorts. I had done research in my field for more than twenty years, and grew up in medical libraries all over the world. I understood research. But I had direct first-hand experience observing this child, *my child*.

*I may only be a foster mom, at least for a little while longer, but I am the only mom this baby has. And so you have to listen to me. You see improved numbers, for which I am also grateful, but I know this baby, and she isn't getting enough air.*

*I am telling you, to feed this baby is a terrifying thing.*

*And I am telling you, this baby turns blue or purple or black multiple times a day, or sometimes not at all. When she is on oxygen, she is a happy and active baby; when she is off oxygen, she is a fussy and sick baby who just lies there panting and getting pneumonia.*

*PRS varies from child to child, from moment to moment, and Kyrie is also unique because of the impact of drug exposure. I know a lot of PRS babies are even sicker than she is, but that doesn't make it okay to leave her failing.*

*At every single appointment she has had, I have said that her development is delayed in spite of what the monitors say, that she is not well despite the results from her sleep studies. But I have been ignored and ignored and ignored — even dismissed as crazy because you don't think what I am saying makes sense. I'm not asking for it to make sense or for you to explain why it is happening. I am telling you what I see, and what every one of her therapists who work with her every week tells me.*

*You don't want to trach her yet, and would rather just re-assess every six weeks, maybe until she is grown. If she is stable, and that's all the intervention she needs, then that's great! No one wants a trach or a G tube. But don't take this very smart baby who cannot move or play, and say she is fine, and then tell me she has cerebral palsy now because you didn't trach her six months ago. If supplemental oxygen is sufficient intervention, then that's simple. But don't say that in the name of research.*

*I am okay with creative problem solving and ingenuity. I know the research of this hospital changes health care all over the world. That's why we are here, because if anyone can do it, you can. But now that you have just shut off two more layers of her airway, you cannot just send us home. I will not put a purple baby in my family van for a three-day road trip. I will not accept purple as our baseline.*

*It's my job to fight for the help she needs, to get her the care that will make her well and healthy and strong, not just alive; we need your care, and we appreciate your care, but we are not interested in you getting paid a hundred grand to play with Tinker Toys.*

I did not shout, though my voice cracked a few times. I was part frustrated, maybe a little angry, and a whole lot scared. But it was a conversation, so we talked. They needed to see her present the symptoms I was describing, not because they didn't believe me, but because they have to be able to document it.

And so she did. They took her off oxygen, and she went dusky in minutes, then suddenly purple, even though she was holding her sats on the monitor. Minutes later her sats also plummeted. Someone finally thought of a similar case, where secretions were part of the problem in a way that didn't show up on the video swallow study. Basically, they decided that besides the airway issues, she was living in a state of drowning, aspirating on her secretions as well as her food.

Drowning I can understand. Whether it's saliva or red tape, it makes it awfully hard to breathe.

# 10

*How am I supposed to hear her at night when I have cochlear implants that need to be charged?*

*How long do the distractors need to be in?*

*When they take them off, will she have to be intubated again?*

*Will the extubation be as horrific as it was the first time, or will it be better because of a bigger airway?*

*How long will she need the NG tube?*

*When will we get to be with our family again?*

These are the things I asked myself and worried about as I paced our tiny room while she slept. I had Hebrew homework I could do, or audio books to listen to, or movies to check out from downstairs, but time ticked by slowly and I couldn't concentrate. I had the concierge pick up a video baby monitor from the store, so I could at least leave our room long enough to go eat in the dining hall, but there wasn't much else to do while her situation was so precarious.

Slipping the video monitor into the pocket of my capris, I silently slipped out of our door in my socks. The afternoon light poured in through the soaring foyer windows as I passed the elevator and headed toward the library. A little girl with no hair bounded out of the door with her rambunctious brother right as I reached for the handle, and we nearly crashed into each other. He laughed and she adjusted the mask covering her face, and they both scampered past me toward the stairs.

Looking for a way to connect to my family back home instead of just being anxious, I fingered the spines of the picture books on the shelves before turning to find a rack full of donated greeting cards. A sign said they were free, so I picked my way through birthday and holiday cards to find ones with funny pictures for my children and sweet ones for Nathan. I sat at a table and wrote each of them a letter, knowing that they would be delighted to receive mail when it arrived.

Addressing their cards eased my longing some, but I was still restless. I couldn't call home from my room while the baby was sleeping, and the open design of the building made it difficult to find a private corner. I stepped back out into the hallway, listlessly circling the second story past the laundry room and coming around to the opposite side. That's when I found the meditation room again, and remembered they had said you can mark it as "occupied" at any time for privacy.

I stepped inside, sliding the sign on the door so that others would know to wait their turn. I closed the door behind me and locked it. There was a softness to the room, muted colors that offered solace compared to the bright palates that cheered the atmosphere downstairs. A fancy leather couch with a heavy coffee table were in the middle of the room. Prayer rugs were rolled in a basket in the corner for those who needed them, and bookshelves on the far side offered a variety of faith-based reading material. A desk faced the window overlooking the downstairs lobby, and an open notebook documented the prayer requests of families who had come before me.

I realized this was the room where parents came to cry. The rest of the building buoyed up families by offering them hope and easing burdens in order to conserve strength. But this room was where parents came to fall apart, to collapse, to fall on their knees and weep.

I realized that the one thing I had, in every moment, even when there is no time to write, no private place to call, and no picture to post on the blog, was simple prayer. I had prayed a lot while we were there, before we had come, before she was born, and I knew many others had prayed for us also. I wanted to pray, and really had been trying, but I was out of words and no longer knew how to ask for help.

I flipped through the notebook softly, feeling intrusive as I read the stories of other parents who had come here. There were public requests for prayer throughout, and that's why it was there, but it still felt like wading in someone else's waters. I read news about cancer, updates about transplants, and information about diagnoses I had never heard of before. I read about the efforts of nurses and doctors, random acts of kindness from strangers, and the difference the hard work of volunteers made in the lives of families staying in that place. I read miracle narratives of blessed children, and brief statements of gratitude for those who passed away instead of getting better, even though God's answer to their prayers had been no.

God had said no when my father died. He said no when my mother was killed. He said no when we lost our other babies. He still heard my prayers in those other times, those times when He said no, those times I grieved until I was turned inside out. He still loved me then, was still mindful of me then, and still knew what was best for me. I knew that Heavenly Father is real, and that He knows us, and that He loves us. He could have said no this time; he didn't, but if he had, my testimony of His love would still be unshaken.

All things – even the no's – work together for the good of those who love Him. That's what Paul said in Romans 8:28. Life had been crazy hard since Nathan and I had gotten married... because we were being transformed. Life was not supposed to be easy and comfortable and quiet, no matter how appealing that seemed. And happiness comes from enduring life together, and being knit together — *sealed* together — through those transformations. We knew His purpose: to bring about the immortality and eternal life of all of us, even me.

As soon as Nathan and I returned home from our honeymoon, still glowing in newly wedded bliss, he hopped a plane back to New York for work just in time for Hurricane Sandy. He was not very worried about the storm, but I was. I tried to stay busy as he banned me from reading Twitter for updates, but I couldn't function enough to do much of my own work. I waited for him to have cell service so that we could FaceTime.

*While you are there fighting off this hurricane, I have been keeping myself busy. I moved my mom, moved three pianos, moved all the furniture, scrubbed the house top to bottom, cleaned the carpets, put the furniture back, and moved more than 450 books.* That's what I thought I might say. Except when my iPad began to ring, what came out of my mouth was, "I'm sorry! I haven't been able to mow the lawn yet!" Stuff and nonsense, such automatic false guilt.

My heart leapt the moment I saw him on screen and knew that he was okay. It was moments like that when you are supposed to be a good wife, radiating strength and courage. So when your husband is stranded in a hurricane, that is not the time for crybaby wives, even when you can imagine water rushing up the stairs. Instead, I did my best just to be present with him in that moment.

There was only so much preparation he could do for a hurricane. He had flashlights, and safe shoes, and water, and food. His phone was charged. The storm moved slowly, and the whole city was stir crazy, waiting for a disaster no one was sure would actually arrive.

And then it did. We watched the news together, checking social media feeds for good pictures and laughing at how people were already spinning the hurricane into funny memes. Once again, we were given a foretaste of what life together would bring — impossible crises that we could only endure by holding hands and laughing our way through.

The next water surges wouldn't come until high tide early in the morning, so he was hoping to sleep a few hours. "You should sleep, too," he said.

"Maybe I will hang pictures a little while," I said.

"Don't forget to eat," he said.

"I have been sick all day," I said.

I slept restlessly, and woke early, needing to keep myself busy to pass the time while I waited for more news from Nathan. I began to obsess about the pool in our backyard that I had won in a work contest earlier that year. It was a tender mercy, because I would rather be in a swimming pool than almost any place else. I had worked hard to take care of it all summer, but I hadn't closed it yet for winter because I had been busy moving my mother into her new rental home around the corner, and finishing my own wedding plans. But now that I was home and settled, it was time to take care of business.

Winterizing, as it turned out, meant adding more chemicals. It's like making a really good stew, except of chemicals. Chemicals you swim in, which made me wonder why I loved swimming so much when I worked so hard to eat organic. When all that was finished, I dragged out the pool cover and unfolded it. It reminded me of playing "parachute" in gym class back in elementary school. I spread it out, and began to pull it up over the side of the pool.

I soon learned what anyone could have told me: that this was not something I could not do by myself. And as usually happens, the more I realized that, the more I took it as a double dog dare to keep trying. I even tied one end of it to the edge of the pool and worked from the opposite side. I almost got it, but then nearly screamed in frustration as it slipped off the other side again, and just rested there in the water, mocking me. I needed to get it done, but there was no one there to help me. It was a new lesson for me, that there were some things I just could not do by myself.

I thought about the day I had (foolishly) put the pool together all by myself, and how hard that was. How much harder could it be just to cover it up? Except I just couldn't get it, and my pride had to accept defeat. I collapsed right there next to my garden, in a pile of girl-tears, and it all came pouring out of me: how I was not as independent as I pretended to be, how being strong wasn't always enough, and how I couldn't make myself busy enough not to miss Nathan or exhausted enough to sleep well without him.

Nathan survived the hurricane just fine, but I became more and more sick in the following weeks. My body was doing weird things, and it confused me. I wondered if I had turned into some kind of Victorian wimp, with fainting spells that kept me from having to do any chores. Conversations with Nathan were a delicious distraction, but even our marital bliss couldn't ease the sickness.

I had been sick since the Monday after Nathan and I got married. Nauseous sick. All-day-long sick. Horrific sick. Even my vertigo was worse than it had been since my cochlear implant surgeries, leaving me dizzy and fainting and crawling along walls to find which way was up.

I ate popcorn at two in the afternoon every day as if it were medicinal, but it wasn't any fun because I was exhausted, confused, and overwhelmed. It was all very irritating. I liked to be up and around, going-going-going, accomplishing anything and everything, and then playing hard to celebrate. Rivers. Parks. Bikes. Running. Gardens. Hands in the dirt. Hair in the wind. That's me. Whiny-puny-wimpy-Emily annoyed me. First a month, then more than a month, then six weeks, and it seemed to be getting worse instead of better.

I had to learn to trust my body, and to listen to it, and to respect it. Even on days that I didn't think we were speaking the same language, my body and I. Nothing seemed to help.

I tried to hide all this from Nathan, but he knew I was sore in strange places and riding waves of nausea. He knew I was swirling in my own emotional hurricane, where everything made me cry more easily than before. I cried when I was happy, sad, confused, or inspired. I cried when he called me, when we said goodbye, when he reminded me that he would be home soon. I cried when I made bread, when I held my puppies, and when I hugged my mom before she left on a trip.

I did finally tell my mom that I was not feeling well. My need for her to be my mom finally overrode my need to protect her from worrying. I told her all of my symptoms, full disclosure. She said what I knew she would: "You need to go to the doctor. You need a new CA-125 blood test. We need to be sure this isn't ovarian cancer like mine was. It's better to be safe than sorry. You are old enough for a mammogram, too. And you can get an ultrasound to be sure everything is okay. Don't mess around with this."

Cancer survivors can be a little intense about following up on random symptoms.

But that's what ovarian cancer is like: random symptoms.

And it's the following up on those symptoms that saves lives.

"I love you," she said.

"I know," I said.

I hugged her goodbye and went to work. I had an appointment already, but I didn't want to worry my family. I didn't tell anyone because I needed to process on my own before the world around me tried to get "helpful". I am stubborn and independent, and it was hard work for me to be receptive to that kind of help. Kindness still seemed shiny and new to me; trust and friendship were skills I was still building. Being social left me exhausted before I even got started.

Late one night, I called and asked Nathan to leave me a voicemail that I could listen to over and over when I missed him and wanted to be close to him. He did. Right away. He called, and left the sweetest message ever. I still listen to it on hard days. He told me I was brave and strong and good, and when he said it I believed it. He said tender things and kind things and funny things. It filled me with love and happiness on a day I was very, very weak. He did this from the streets of New York, late at night, by the subway, where people notice if you stop in the middle of people-traffic, where you can get mugged for pulling out your phone on the street, where strangers could overhear his words to me. That is a bold man, unafraid to love, and doing everything he could to stay connected from so far away.

It turns out that if you get married and even sneeze the next day, all your friends and church family giggle because they think you might be pregnant. My friends noticed my food aversion, saw my vertigo knock me flat when I tried to stand, and watched nausea wash over me whenever I moved. They asked me if I was "late". I reminded them that I am always late, but they ignored my joke, urging me to take a home pregnancy test. I dismissed them, explaining that it took my parents almost ten years to be able to have children.

As soon as the words came out of my mouth, everything around me seemed to blur into the background while I stood under my own internal spotlight. *We don't have ten years*, I thought, considering another impact of waiting until later in life to marry. I pushed this thought out of my head immediately, because it was a grief I could not bear to ponder. I gave in to my friends and let them distract me, and I took the pregnancy test the next morning.

I learned how terrifying it is for just the thought of pregnancy to come into your head, even when you are excited and understand doctrine and are willing to learn some family love. When my test was negative, I also learned that it's confusing when you feel okay with what should have been disappointment, but also still sad in a way.

My friends told me to wait two more days, and take the test again. I took it again, and then again, and then again. Married for only six weeks, I already hated pregnancy tests. I hated waiting for a tiny little window to tell me what I already knew. I hated that it argued with me. I hated the hope, and the disappointment. I hated the roller coaster. I hated the waiting. I hated the waiting. I hated the waiting.

I hated that it didn't have a window that said "cancer" or "not cancer". I could endure the waiting, even relish in the sacred secret of a new pregnancy, if it were not for the cancer factor. This was not some tender moment shared with an attentive husband. We were not waiting for the good news of a miracle baby; we were ruling out cancer. I hated that cancer got a role in what should have been a moment of joy. I hated that cancer got to invade all the most precious moments of our lives. I hated that cancer attacked my mom while I was away from home so long ago, and that cancer killed my dad just the year before.

I didn't even care about the stupid test (negative again), and threw it against the wall when my three minutes were up. I was angry at cancer, angry at death, angry at emotions that were overriding my brain. I curled up on the cold floor, my face against the wall, needing to pray but having no words. Some prayers are only tears, and some prayers are only breaths.

The floor was cold and hard, and my body stiff. Nausea swept over me again, and I scooted closer to the toilet. When it finally passed, I moved to the carpeted floor of the adjoining closet, covering myself with a childhood blanket. I knelt there, my head between my knees from feeling dizzy as much as in effort to pray.

I thanked Heavenly Father for answering my prayers so exactly, for giving me a husband, and for sending me one who would do the hard work to truly be alive in loving. I thanked Him for the protection we had in all our travels back and forth, and in our time apart. I thanked Him for provision, for all that had been given to us, for our temporal needs being met, and for spiritual blessings overflowing. I thanked Him for challenging me in the ways that allowed me to grow me in the ways I needed. I thanked Him for knowing me so well, for loving me so much, for being both my Father and my God.

*I repent of being afraid.*

*I am ashamed, and I am sorry.*

Only then did I start to see clearly. I sat up. I blew my nose. I waited. I prayed, and quietly waited for answers.

Just then, the man who performed our marriage — the sealing ordinance for Nathan and me in the temple — sent me a text message, reminding me that this was the pattern of my life: to be tested by big and scary things, and that when I faced them with faith, the miracle always followed. He said, "Do not be afraid."

Then, the man who spoke at our wedding reception sent me a message with his wife, telling me that God knew what Nathan and I needed for the most blessings specific to us, and acting in faith for this meant *not being afraid*, that only then could we move forward in confidence before the Lord.

I was in awe at their timing, and knew that God always offers two witnesses of truth, which confirmed to me that these messages were tender mercies from the Lord. I also knew that, unknowingly, they were quoting my patriarchal blessing: *Do not be afraid. Move forward with this great gift of faith...* But while I was trying hard not to be afraid, I did not yet feel brave.

My appointment was with a new doctor I hadn't even met yet. But he had good news for me: It was not cancer. My tumor markers were still high, but holding steady. It was like being on pause, as if the cancer couldn't win until I fulfilled some purpose, and yet it wouldn't quite go away. I imagined myself growling at it, forcing it back into the shadows. *No cancer today. Not yet. Not today.*

There was also other news: I was, indeed, pregnant.

*Pregnant.*

Except nothing ever happens the easy way.

I numbly listened to his explanation, wanting to be relieved by my cancer results, and trying to be excited about pregnancy, but I was interrupted by the rest of his report. It was physically painful, that pinball of emotions. I couldn't keep up as the words droned past my computer ears. Blighted Ovum. There was a placenta sac, but the baby was not developing. He said we could do a D&C and "get it over with". I told him I read the D&C every morning, but that's a pretty bleak Mormon in-joke, and he didn't understand. He said we could also wait, because it could just be "a baby taking his time". *That's so us.* He said it might just be too early to see clearly. We needed a different kind of ultrasound. We could wait a few weeks and look again, he said, but the risk was that if the baby did not develop, I would miscarry. Most people, he said, like to do the D&C so as to avoid the miscarriage, which can be "messy".

*I need a new doctor,* I thought to myself.

I looked at him and said, "Families are messy. Children are messy. It's part of the deal."

He just blinked.

He told me to make a follow-up appointment in a few weeks, but I bypassed the appointment desk on my way back to the car.

I wanted to talk with Nathan, and called him on the phone. He agreed: we would not end a pregnancy "just to get it over with", not if there was even a small chance everything was fine. It was so early, our baby such a tiny fleck, how could they find it yet anyway? We were quiet together, in awe that we had created something, in awe that we were married, in awe that so much was happening so fast. Then we started to giggle a little, because everybody was gonna know we made us a baby.

The morning was fine, and for one morning I was happy, without tears, and at peace, because I had a testimony of my own child.

But in the afternoon, the pains began.

New pains, pains in my belly, and pains in my back, unlike any other cramping I had ever felt.

I tried to rest. I tried to be still. I was afraid, and did not want to move, not even to cry. If I could be careful enough, then I could be in control; if I could be still enough, then this child would not slip from me so soon. I tried to feel anything there was to feel, desperately needing to feel something, knowing it was too early to feel anything, and afraid that I might feel nothing.

I knew my body was ready to let go, that it was going to release my child without my permission.

But I was not ready.

There was a new kind of waiting, when one day at a time turns into one minute at a time, pleading and waiting, hoping and waiting, not breathing and waiting. Waiting, waiting, waiting. Seconds stretched like weeks. *Nathan will be home in the morning. Everything will be okay when he gets here.* The waiting got harder when pains came again, when cramping grew worse, when my body screamed its first drops of blood. I tried not to move at all, not even to breathe, as if that would hold everything inside me. I tried as if I could save that tiny Lima-bean-sized parasite-child through my own sheer force of will, and begged Heavenly Parents to let me keep that baby.

The answer was no.

When Nathan arrived home, I wrapped my arms tightly around him, as if I were holding a piece of what I had just lost. I cried through the blessing he gave me, and as we knelt together to thank our God for allowing us the opportunity to host a child into mortality, even though we were not called to raise him at that time. I cried as we thanked our Father for that righteous spirit that had come as a part of our family. I cried as we acknowledged our understanding of what He was asking of us, even letting this one go.

All along, there had not been happiness or glowing, but only distress and violent sickness. It would be the same with five more miscarriages. I understood in a new way how and why a mother would endure anything for her child.

After a month of more than forty blood tests done on our eight vials of extracted goop, and all the waiting that followed, we finally got our fertility results. The doctor told us it would be two weeks of waiting, and then we would come up with a treatment plan for how to proceed.

Only that's not what happened.

She got the results, and called us, and instead of telling us results or giving us options over the phone, she told us we needed to have a meeting in person to talk about the tests. That never feels good coming from a doctor. We knew it was bad news, and bad enough she wanted to tell us in person. We braced for that day. We tried to be prepared. We knew a hit was coming. But it still felt like a sucker punch.

There was some good news about everything working in our brains, she said: all the signals going from our brains to our organs were as they should be and working properly. In fact, in both of us, our brains were telling our bodies as loudly as they could that they should be doing all that reproductive stuff.

But that's part of the problem, she said: our brains should be just whispering. "We always whisper to little tiny babies, so your brain should just be whispering to all those parts that make a baby, to all those parts that take care of the parts that make a baby." Our brains are screaming, she said. "That means your brains know something is wrong, so they are trying really hard to make sure the signal gets there. But it just isn't working."

My results showed what we already feared, that my past treatments for ovarian cancer had affected my eggs enough that not many had survived. The few remaining eggs were good quality, so we still had a tiny, microscopic chance of a healthy pregnancy, but not enough of them remained for en vitro fertilization.

"These blood levels here," she said, pointing to a chart, "I call them babysitters. They are the babysitters around each egg, and when they are working hard nourishing and nurturing an egg to maturity, they send off a signal that everything is going okay. But when the egg is damaged or has already died, they don't have to work hard. There's no sweat. There's no signal back to the brain that everything is okay. Because it's not okay."

Nathan was next, and she said, "These sperm just aren't shaped right. They are supposed to fit the egg like a lock and key, and these are not going to unlock anything." Then she added a football analogy for my musical theater husband, telling him, "These guys have to swim five football fields, and only one is going to make it, and he forgot his keys." This double whammy, it turns out, is what caused our miscarriages: eggs damaged by chemo and sperm that don't play football.

We walked slowly back to our car, in another moment where there were no words because there was no air. He unlocked the door, opened it for me, and tucked in my skirt before kissing me on the forehead. The mirror image of me in the window glass fought back tears in sunshine that burned, and I gulped for air as Nathan slowly climbed into the car. He took my hand, and we held each other. Tears came for the children we would not have, for how hard we tried, for those we lost, for those we thought we lost, and for the year of grief we had. Nathan whispered another prayer for us, and we sat there together in silence for a very long time.

We were both startled when the phone rang. We were more startled when we saw who was calling: Department of Human Services. "We have a boy," a woman said, "a little boy needs placement in a foster home. Do you still want to do this?" Nathan and I looked at each other. This timing was either cruel or a tender mercy, and we needed to choose mercy. We said yes, igniting the firestorm of three years as foster parents.

Our first foster placement was only for respite care, and he was scheduled to return to his official foster home after ten days. They said his case was so challenging that the foster family needed a break. He was five, and was just out of full body casts for broken arms and broken ribs and broken legs. His paperwork wasn't untangled yet, so we didn't get paid that first time, but he had already been in custody in the hospital and so came with some clothes and toys. We borrowed a bike from a family at church, and another family gave us some toy cars, and we went out and bought his favorite movie.

We were *terrified*. We knew we would have to jump in at some point, but this was one of the worst cases of abuse I had heard of even from two decades of clinical work as a counselor. He arrived on Nathan's birthday, with brown hair and big eyes, looking very proud of himself in bright green cowboy boots.

We felt a little jumpy with the young mystery, not wanting to trigger him and fearing we would be unprepared for how to help. We were all three like tigers in a cage, circling around each other, getting to know each other, waiting to see who was going to make the first move. He didn't take his eyes off us, even when he pretended to play.

He didn't really know how to play, anyway. He just mimicked us as we tried to show him how to build blocks and race Matchbox cars. He was loud, talking constantly to assess where we were and what we were doing and what we were thinking. He was on the offense, making sure he was safe, trying to predict what we were going to do next. It was intrusive and exhausting. Everything in my bones screamed to take off my cochlear implant processors, to make it stop, to come up for air, but listening was exactly what he needed. Eye contact and interaction were the only ways he knew he was safe. So we listened, and made no sudden moves, and he talked and talked and talked. And asked a hundred questions. And then talked some more.

Meals were difficult. He only ate ketchup or peanut butter sandwiches that he made himself, and which he hoarded at night. We made a plan to let him keep one in a special basket by his bed to feel safe. We left out apples and a sandwich during the day, so that he could have some whenever he wanted without asking permission. That way he knew he really would get food at our house, and knew that it was his, even though we also modeled regular meal times.

When he got scared, he acted angry towards the dogs. We ended up bringing them in whenever he went to play outside. We had heard stories of his aggression, but he wasn't with us long enough to act out towards Nathan or me.

He didn't have any parental visits while he was with us, but his foster family showed up one day unexpectedly. They rang the doorbell, and when we opened it, all of his things were on the porch and they were driving off. We called the caseworker, but it took weeks before he could convince the kinship family they had to take him back.

Over the time that he was with us, there seemed to be a shift in his behavior. He tried really hard to please us: he became more polite, more interested in church, and helpful around the house. We spoke with him about how, when he went back to the environment of his other home, it would be hard for him to maintain those positive changes. But when we drove him there, and spent some time talking with his caregivers, we watched him interact with the other children there. His behavior changed like a chameleon, transforming him into a boy we didn't even recognize. It was heartbreaking not to know whether there was any reality to the kind-hearted boy we had come to know. We have worried about him since, that unwanted boy who got sent back to nowhere.

We couldn't save every child, but we kept trying as if we could.

# 11

Five weeks after being Life-Flighted to Cincinnati, four weeks since surgery, and one week since she woke from the coma, Kyrie was finally cleared by plastics for me to stop turning her distractors. Her jaw had moved out so far that her tongue had finally popped out of her throat and into place where it should be, opening the upper part of her airway. The doctor wanted her to "cook" for a week with the distractors still in position, but not turning further, and he said that taking them out would be as simple as just snipping the bars inside her mouth and pulling them out of her face. "In other countries," he said, "they do it bedside because it is so simple. If she can keep breathing and only be sedated, it will be quick and easy, but needing to intubate her would make things more difficult."

Kyrie had not been able to close her mouth or swallow while her jaw was propped open by the distractors, but they had not sent anything for me to clean or moisten her mouth when they discharged her. It was another example of the doctors being overly focused on their own specialty and not thinking about the whole child. Aggressively proud of their ability to shove bars through her face in order to restructure it, they didn't consider the fact that her mouth and tongue would become very dry and uncomfortable when stuck open for so many weeks. I had tried my best with the resources I had, but now that we were back in the hospital and I had access to mouth sponges, she was obviously relieved.

I could see her new chin sticking out, since she had grown almost three inches of jaw in a month. I would not be able to know what her new face shape looked like until after the distractors came out. The plastics doctor said her bones were still so soft that he would be able to shape her like Play-Doh.

Once again, she and I spent some very sacred time together the night before surgery. It would be risky enough that the nurses kept telling me to say my farewells, just in case. They took off all her tubes and wires (except the NG tube) and let me give her a real bath in a tub. They let me wash her hair for real, wash her body with a washcloth, dry her with a baby towel, and massage her with lotion. They let me clean her pin sites for the distractors, clean out her mouth, and put balm on her little lips. They let me hold her while they reconnected her, then let me dress her in her surgery gown, swaddle her in the hospital blanket, and rock her for a very long time.

Each time I gave Kyrie one of these pre-surgery baths, the nurses thought I was saying goodbye, that I was preparing her in case she died. But I knew that I was washing the hospital off of her, anointing her with prayer, and empowering her with love and blessings so that she could receive the promises of being sealed in the temple. *Everything is going to be okay*, I promised. I combed her curls, and tucked her in, and held her feeding tube up above her head for her dinner. Then I sang her to sleep and kissed her good night. I said her bedtime prayer, turned out the light, and let her rest.

Surgery could be any time after six in the morning. Her medicine would keep her asleep until then. I needed to return to RMHC for my first full night's sleep in six weeks, and to care for myself. I also didn't want to stay in the room and keep disturbing her with my own anxiety.

I whispered to her again before I left. *Everything is going to be okay.* But I didn't promise her that it would be easy, or that it wouldn't be a scary couple of months ahead. She deserved to know the truth and have her experience validated, even if she was only a baby.

I slipped out of her room, around the corner, down the hallway, and waited by the elevator. I thought about how often it had been that our family had no answers, that we hadn't known if things would turn out okay. I remembered how Anber had begun randomly flipping out during visits with her mother that second summer, when she normally would have been happily playing on the playground. She had grown wary of her mother, and the caseworker and I couldn't figure out what the trigger was. Anber started running away from her mother, or even picking fights with her on visits. It turned out that Anber knew before anyone else that her mother was using heroin again. I learned then to trust a child, even when they were too young to verbally express what they already understood.

I rode the elevator down to the main floor of the hospital, stepping out past the security guards by the front desks. The hot summer air hit me as I came out the front doors of the hospital and found a bench on which to rest while I waited for the shuttle back to RMHC. I kept thinking about Kyrie, and her half-sister Anber, Alex, Mary, Kirk, and Barrett, and how we could not undo what they had already endured. No matter how well we loved them, or how hard we tried to treat them well, we could not change what had already happened to them.

We could make this life now be safe and predictable and fun and happy. We could teach them about choices and consequences, and about love and kindness. We could tell them not to do drugs, and hope they would choose wisely. We could even tell them that their biological families love them so much, and explain how addictions make it so that people lose their ability to make choices for themselves. We could emphasize that we were really, really happy we got the chance to love them. We could tell them every day that they are beloved children of Heavenly Parents, and that they were noble and valiant spirits premortally, and that we are honored to live in their presence.

I climbed onto the shuttle when it arrived, collapsing onto a seat. I stared out the window as we waited at the light, watching busy people go by. The people heading toward the hospital looked afraid, and the people leaving the hospital looked exhausted. It reminded me of changes in children when they first come into foster care.

When visits with biological family first start, there is a re-opening of wounded hearts with each hello and each goodbye, and then a different gradual change that comes over them when those visits finally stop. I remembered how, early on, the children that stayed would blurt out things like, "My daddy beat me" or, "My mother's in jail for stealing." Nathan and I would awkwardly try to clarify that they weren't talking about us. But over time, those pieces would heal, or scar over, or go into hiding to pop out later. We once had a young toddler placed with us, and a year later when she began to talk, her first sentence was, "You can make $600 a day from meth." It took some time for conversation to shift to new memories and experiences we had made together as a family.

When it was appropriate, we read stories to our children about termination of parental rights, and found books about adoption for them. We wanted them to have the lingo in their vocabulary as they grew, so they would better understand what had happened to them. We didn't hide from tough subjects like addiction, abuse, and pornography, robbing those shadows of power over our children's lives by shining a light on them.

As the shuttle pulled into the circle drive in front of the RMHC building, I felt the presence of my parents near me, as if they were whispering, "Everything is going to be okay. That is the promise of the temple." I knew it was true, and it made me smile to know that my parents and even my ancestors, knew it, too. We had come so far to understand this. Both my parents passed through the veil early enough to meet this baby girl before she was born. I even felt whispers from my children's children, not yet born but so very real and present. *Everything is going to be okay.*

I didn't know when the scene changed to some kind of Fred Astaire black-and-white haze. It began with music, far-away music that made me stretch and move and dance, searching for Nathan to embrace me for a spin around the floor. The music got louder and louder, but the mist got thicker, and I felt pulled away from Nathan by the weight of having to squeeze back into my mortal body. Then I realized I was somewhere between waking and dreaming, and far too tired to make my body stir. I tried to wake, but my eyes were too heavy to open. My eyes fluttered when my brain came back online, realizing I had managed to sleep with my cochlear implants on again, and that the music I was hearing was my phone alarm. *7 Keys* by Aqualung. It was our wedding dance song.

I had to have myself ready by five in the morning, for Kyrie to be ready by six. There were two delays as we waited her turn for surgery, which meant keeping her occupied (and not thinking about food) any way we could. When they finally came for her, I kissed her goodbye and watched as they whisked that jail-faced baby away from me once again.

When I was called back to the recovery room before I even had time to finish my breakfast, I was so startled that I knocked over my drink and spilled yogurt on the floor. I held my breath, trying not to run back to her recovery station, following the paw print stickers on the floor through a zig-zag of hallways and curtains to her bed. A nurse was there, holding Kyrie, and turned to pass her to me. That was the first moment I ever got to cradle her like a real baby in my arms, instead of up on my shoulder for her to breathe. She was finally set free from her hardware, and *oh! That precious face!*

We didn't fall hopelessly in love with each and every one of the children who came through our home. We loved them, sure, but sometimes that love was the product of hard labor and sacrifice. With some, we actually breathed sighs of relief when they left. Those children did not much like us, either, and we learned that sometimes part of a good placement was just matching personalities well — which got harder as the number of people in our home grew.

When we were still new foster parents, and every departure was a formal event, I once called a family meeting in preparation for sending off a precocious seven-year-old girl. Wildly creative, and equally clumsy, we weren't sure the world that she saw through those Coke-bottle glasses was the same one the rest of us lived in. Feeling very proud of my mothering skills, I asked her to share with us three things that she had learned during her time with us. Her response made me spew water out my nose:

"Number One: BORING!

"Number Two: Why am I even here?

"Number Three: How to say grace."

On the whole, we considered that a win.

Another little girl, a toddler, was supposed to be with us long-term, and we were asked to start considering adoption, although parental rights had not yet been terminated. However, even at that young age, it felt as if she was not choosing us back, that she did not want us to adopt her. We always took a lot of pictures in our family, in part, to document children's experiences for their biological parents, but after more than a year, we did not have even one group photo without her crawling or running out of the shot, literally trying to get away from us as fast as she could. It seemed impossible that she could understand or make a choice like that at such a young age, but it also seemed a consistent preference that we needed to respect. Eventually, she was placed back with her mother, but re-entered foster care three more times, so that we had several tries together as a family, but it was never a match. When she came back into foster care the last time, we declined the placement so that she would have other opportunity to find her forever family.

Letting babies leave is never easy, even when you know their new home is good and safe. The first foster baby we had in the home after my cancer was a sick one, and I stayed with her in the hospital in Tulsa for several weeks. That experience helped prepare me for Kyrie, I am sure. This one had blonde hair and bright eyes, and we called her Golden. Like many drug babies, she was too tiny to fit in newborn or even preemie clothes, so I dressed her in baby doll outfits. When we finally brought her home, all the children were smitten with her immediately.

I loved that baby so much, and our bond was unique from the many other babies we had cared for, so when they found her grandparents, letting her go was rough. It was maybe harder to say goodbye to Golden, than letting go of any of the others. We got to see her again, though, because the grandparents used us several times as babysitters. I was able to make my peace with saying goodbye again and again, because we knew she was loved and spoiled by good grandparents.

That golden baby will not remember me, even though her picture still hangs on my wall. This child will not know me when she sees me again, even though I have thought of her every single day since she left my home. This child will not know we saved her life, or bought her clothes, or fed her, or let her poop in our lap. She will not remember the songs that we sang, or what we smelled like, or how we sounded. She won't know I was the first one to hear her little voice coo, or the first one to see her smile, or that I caught her rolling over for the first time on video. She won't know I took her picture in a rocking chair, on an ancient sofa, or in a glass bowl. She won't know the story of the weeks we spent together in the hospital, or how I didn't sleep so she could stay alive, or how her tiny fingers held mine while she slept with tubes flowing out of her. She won't remember my name, or that she was here, or that she used to turn to find me when she heard my voice enter a room. She won't remember that I cried when I held her and said goodbye.

I pretended that the clothes I sent with her were like hugs, even if she didn't know they were from me. I pretended the instructions I gave the grandparents from the hospital would keep her healthy and strong. I pretended they would follow the safety plan and keep her alive. I hoped, and have to believe, that there was something of our Spirit that she would retain, in some way, like a faint memory, and that maybe it would keep her looking beyond her circumstances and help her overcome her rough start in mortality. I hoped, and had to believe, that someday she might hear our lullaby songs somewhere, and that they would be familiar enough to her to feel like a clue to something good and peaceful and safe. I hoped, and had to believe, that the priesthood blessing that Nathan gave her was real, and that taking her to the temple, even just to touch it with her tiny hand, will mean something, and that the spirit I saw in her will still be the girl I see again someday.

Saying goodbye to a foster child always had another meaning as well: it meant an empty bed, a waiting room, and the anticipation of seeing who would be next. *When would they call us? What would the story be? How many siblings? How old would they be?*

One night I went in to tuck Alex into bed, and he said that Heavenly Father told him a new boy was coming to sleep in his bunk bed. So he asked me to be sure and let the boy sleep in the bottom bunk, so that he wouldn't fall. I promised, kissed his red head, and tucked him in before sneaking out to the hallway. Nathan and I laughed about it later, but the next day, we got a call for a three-year-old boy. He came just long enough to take a nap for three hours in Alex's bed before a kinship placement was found, and he moved on that quickly.

Once, a new foster boy getting used to his new kindergarten class announced at dinner that he wasn't going to be allowed any doughnuts at a school party.

I asked him, "Why not?"

"I don't have a dad for doughnut day."

"Can Nathan go with you, for substitute-dad doughnut day?"

"I think the police busted my dad for drugs, and I might not see him again."

Nathan did go to substitute-dad doughnut day, and was treated to the sight of this boy squirting puddles of mustard onto the cafeteria table, and then slurping them up. It was not the heart-warming bonding experience that he had expected.

When a new sibling group of four had joined Alex and Anber in our home, they were looking at faded family photos on the piano and asked me, "Who is this little girl?"

"That was my mama when she was a little girl."

"Why don't you have a little girl?"

"I have two of you! And three boys, look at you!"

"We might go home tomorrow. Or next year."

"We will see what happens."

"So, are you sad to have no kids and only dead parents?"

It's a question that stings, and it stings because it is a real question. The clinical supervisor for my counseling license was a Jungian, and I learned from him that real questions are often harder than real answers. These children have lived hard, and so they know better than anyone how to ask real questions.

Discussing this incident, I asked Nathan, "Do you think that people on the other side of the veil remember us? Or do they start to forget our faces after a time?"

He patted me on the shoulder, "You've been listening to *Yentl* again, haven't you?"

"I miss my parents."

"You are a masochist."

The hardest emotional moment in fostering for me, though, was the first time I had to go to court in the town where the ambulance took my mother to die. I didn't want to go. Nathan told me I didn't have to if I didn't want to, but if I did, I could pick up the hospital records we needed while I was there, so that all of it would be over and finished.

"Finished, like expired?" I asked. *Papa, please forgive me. Try to understand me. Mama, don't you know I had no choice?*

We already knew Alex and Anber were staying, and that Mary was with us long-term, though it was perpetually uncertain whether she would be able to be adopted. When we found out Anber was having a sister, Alex began feeling out-numbered as the only boy. His solution to this was to start praying up some brothers again. This time he even told us that Heavenly Father had revealed some specific details to help us find them: that one was his age and the other was younger, that one was gentle but the other was a screamer, and that Alex himself would have to change beds to accommodate their special needs.

Sometime later, our adoption worker came by with paperwork to officially move Alex from foster status to adoptive placement. She said that she knew a couple of boys who were already legally free for adoption, but who would be difficult to place because the older boy had cerebral palsy. She had thought of us, she said, because of the funny things we had told her about Alex's brother-prayers. An immediate and irrational conviction came to us that we needed these boys. We were cautious, however, because we had thus far only fostered, and these brothers would specifically be placed with us for adoption.

It was a big step for us as family. We knew the critical piece was seeing how the children interacted, and whether these two surprises could mesh well with our long-termers. It wouldn't be fair to Alex or Anber or Mary if a change was too disruptive, and the brothers had been through enough placements already that we didn't want to invite them here only for them to have to move again. We came up with a plan for a very slow transition, to be sure all the children were comfortable with the idea before doing anything official.

Our first play date was at a local park, where we met one morning just to get to know each other. We were immediately struck by how much Kirk, the older brother, looked like a miniature Nathan, even down to the matching glasses. We loved how Barrett, the younger brother, could hold his own with Anber and even keep up with Alex. They were both sweet boys, and friendships among the children took off immediately.

Kirk and Barrett were very vocal about their history, and would often share new details at unexpected moments, like sad little Easter eggs. They described a history of abuse from boyfriends living with their biological mother. Their mother had left Kirk's father, but continued the pattern of domestic violence with Barrett's father. The brothers described being given alcohol, seeing people doing drugs, and "lots of screaming and hitting and throwing things." Kirk's most traumatic memory, one that still haunts him some nights and one that he bravely faces every Saturday when we do his laundry together, was being thrown into the dryer and locked inside. Barrett was only six months old when they were taken into state custody, so, like Anber, his memories of that early life are cloudy. But, also like Anber, he often acts out early pre-verbal memories in his aggressive rough-housing, and still screams threats of violence when he is angry.

Kirk's cerebral palsy requires braces for both legs and on his left arm. Due to hydrocephalus, he also has a shunt from his head to his heart, to keep the fluid from building up in his brain. Barrett's fetal alcohol syndrome has left him struggling with his emotions, so that he was with us nearly a year before he was able to express sadness or anger without screaming how he wanted to cut off our heads or set our beds on fire. He was three-and-a-half when he came to us, and still in diapers. We got him potty-trained really quick.

We started having regular play dates in the evenings and on weekends, and it was a fascinating thing to watch the children get to know each other. Kirk got wobbly when he was tired, but tried everything and did not give up easily. He had a sweet spirit and was super tender to the little ones, while getting along famously with Alex — understanding each other in a way no one else ever has. When he got too tired to keep up with Alex, Mary and Kirk had fun playing quieter games. Barrett could always keep up with Alex, giving him a run for his money after a year of mostly foster sisters. Those two ran like crazy, laughing hysterically, and this seemed to be the best therapy for both of them.

"Dating" the boys went well over several weeks, so we started keeping them all day on Saturdays, then for overnights on Fridays, and then all weekend for several weeks in a row. The boys finally moved in after that, and everything went very smoothly. It was a beautiful experience of direct adoptive placement. We felt heavenly whispers telling us they were ours, the same way we felt them when Alex and Anber and Mary came.

That's how we got triplets and twins, quite on accident. Mary, Alex, and Kirk were all six years old at the time — what could go wrong with three sixes? Barrett and Anber were both three. Five children, plus Kyrie still on the way, was more than we ever imagined, especially when we had gotten married just three years before. Having so many children in the same age range was even more of a challenge to our parenting skills. Six plates of food needed cutting; twelve little shoes needed tying; and oh, the laundry!

We were in love with them, and each child seemed to fit our puzzling family in some unique way. Adoption itself seemed a very smooth and easy transition once it was time. It was terrifying, since we'd had little time to learn to be parents of so many, and it seemed that we had to apologize for our own bad behavior just as often as the children had to apologize for their squabbles amongst each other. But there we were, learning together, creating a family, declaring order from the chaos.

It was ironic that it was our job to mentor biological parents when we really had no idea what we were doing. We were slow to realize that fostering put us on the accelerated parent training plan, demanding both skills and newly found confidence. When one mother asked how we had turned her angry baby into such a happy toddler, I didn't know how to explain it to her. *Limit-setting. Boundaries. Consistency. Nurture. Love. Cuddles. Food. Milk. Songs. Stories. Playtime. Blocks. Blankets. Clothes that fit. Regular sleep. Stimulation. Learning. Practice doing things. Time to be a child.* What seemed common sense to us was all together unfamiliar to them, often because they themselves had never been parented well.

Another time, we fortified an out-of-state grandmother with all the details of the routine we had been using with the preschooler sibling set that was heading her way. When the children were finally flown to her for placement, she worked hard to implement the things we taught her. She was surprised they had learned to say prayers at bedtime, and said it had become a special experience for her, as it revealed so much about what was in their little heads at the end of the day. We had been willing to adopt those children, when we were asked, but in the end, were glad they were able to go home to family who wanted and loved them.

It was a tricky thing, adopting some and not others. Some did not want to be adopted, and others got sent home after we thought they would be adopted. Others watched foster siblings get adopted while waiting on their own court updates and wanting to know what would happen to them. Mary was one of those. We were careful to give her extra support and attention so she didn't feel left out, even finding ways she could participate in her own process, like starting to make her adoption video. She wanted closure, but we could not fix everything, or wrap it up in a shiny ribbon like a thirty-minute sitcom.

Life is harder than that, and rarely do things go smoothly in the life of a foster child. We weren't sure whether we should be delighted or horrified when Mary's mother offered to relinquish her parental rights in exchange for some white cheese dip at the Mexican place in town. We told her that she probably should talk to her attorney about that, and that we didn't think we were really allowed to make deals. Children are not up for negotiation.

In the end, after Mary had lived with us for two whole years, Mary's mother and father both signed her over to the state voluntarily. When we gave Mary the news, it was the first time she shared stories about her biological father, telling us he was in prison. We knew the charges were for domestic violence, but Mary added that she had been hit and thrown against a wall, and that he had pulled her mother across the floor by her hair. Since telling us that story, Mary has consistently reported that is how she lost her hearing. "My ears worked until that day," she says, "and then, when I hit that wall, my ears just turned off."

Even after relinquishment, when things should have been quick and easy, her path to adoption was complicated. Paperwork was missing. Her child profile, a complete case history that is filled out for each adoptee, took months longer than expected to be completed. All that had to be finished before she could even get in line for a court date. Even once we had a court date, she didn't entirely believe us, after waiting for so long, that it was actually happening.

Sometimes you choose your stories, like agreeing to sign up for fostering. Other times, you just have to wait to see how your story will play out. After their first three months with us, Alex finally started calling his teacher by her name instead of calling her mom, and Anber began asking to be held on sleepy mornings. With practice, Mary picked up on sign language so well she didn't need her cochlear implants or any voiced words to express her active mind with her hands. Kirk learned to open doorknobs with his weaker left hand, and Barrett figured out that his big screaming trigger was being hungry "because baby Barrett didn't always have enough milk." Gradually, our story became one with more laughing, fewer tantrums, more hugs, fewer fistfights, and we slowly (ever so slowly) made progress in becoming a family.

# 12

I walked in the steamy sun, the air hot from summer but the trees wet from rain. I slipped my Crocs sandals off, resting them on the top of the stroller as I weaved my bare feet through the zoo. My toes grazed the blacktop surface of the walking path. The ground was warm, but did not burn me because water was pooling in small dips in the pavement. When the breeze stirred, I held my face to it, filling my own lungs with breath and letting it refresh my spirit as it blew through my short hair still growing back from chemo.

Kyrie was too young to notice animals or details of the exhibit, but it was good for both of us to breathe outside air, to fill our eyes with color, and to surround ourselves with the sounds of life instead of only beeping machines. The contrast was stark, making me realize how worn out we were from the last few weeks, but also aware of how isolated we had been in our sterile world. The Cincinnati Zoo was gorgeous, with what seemed like fences of flowers dancing in the foreground, while the full canopy of a thousand shades of green hung overhead. It was like visiting a temple, a moment of worship, inhaling creation instead of stale air.

I couldn't help but sing as I walked, and my singing made Kyrie laugh. Laughing was new for her, and I don't know how she managed it with such a sore face. The support strap still wrapped around her head like the bandage around Jacob Marley's face in *A Christmas Carol*.

She had also started making a funny gurgle sound after so many days of talking to peacocks on our morning walks at the zoo. It made everyone who heard it laugh, and it gave me a glimpse into her emerging personality. Her spirit was bigger than her tiny body, and she somehow had a gift of connecting to people with her eyes. It was bigger than just charming them; she somehow brought them joy, and peace, and love — even to strangers she met along our walks. She stopped people in their tracks, and they couldn't help but stare into her eyes, hypnotized, and then stand there giggling and laughing while she babbled at them. She gave them hope somehow, these people we didn't know and who had no idea of her own incredible story.

Our walks began from our upstairs room at RMHC, down the elevator, around the ramp by the playground, and down the sidewalk to the zoo just down the street. We entered as pedestrians through the educational building at the back of the zoo, walked the main paths, and picked up lunch for me before heading back up the hill to the hospital. It was just enough of a walk to keep my body strong and my lymph system flushed out, but not too much to be hard on me or her. It became a part of our routine, passing the time between outpatient appointments and counting the days until we could go home.

The hospital is a very different experience on an outpatient basis. As much as the airway unit team worked to make us comfortable and keep her calm, the clinic aspect of the hospital bustled with activity and noise. The nurses we had grown to love and appreciate were still busy on their units, and we were checked in and out by strangers falling in love with Kyrie for the first time. We got to work with the same two speech-path ladies, but everyone else was new. Kyrie was wary of them — and their green gloves — but still recognized the chaplains immediately.

We had primarily seen two chaplains during our stay: one had sung to her in Hebrew, and the other had hummed us back to life during extubation. The hospital had a lovely chapel area, with separate sections for different faith groups or general use. Kyrie brightened when we visited there, seeing the lines and colors and soft light. I think she knew it was a healing place.

It reminded me, of course, of the chapels I had left back home. Nearing the end of my Clinical Pastoral Education (CPE) units for chaplain training, I had spent many hours alone in hospital chapels praying for those I had visited, preparing sermons for services, or silently pleading for comfort to grieving families as I spoke at funerals. I had even recorded some hymns, me either singing or playing them on my cello, and these I now sent home for the children to remember my voice and feel loved from a thousand miles away.

When I had first interviewed for admission into the CPE program, I was asked what in my life had brought me to choose chaplaincy. I had told them that I met my first hospital chaplain when my father was dying, and the idea called to me as an opportunity to integrate my past experiences with grief with service to others.

I felt like the past five years had been so crammed with experiences of death that my internal dialogue had been very focused on survival. I felt as if I was cold, sitting in the unending rain, waiting for the storm to pass. Sometimes it was worse, like I was lying low under a train that was going over me, and all I could hear was the loud clackety racket of the wheels that threatened to crush me. I had no control over it, and could do nothing to make it go away.

The train had faded into the distance over the last year, and the sun began to warm me once again. In my mind, I waded through mud to get out into the light, but could not do more than that yet. The years had been hard, and terrible, and I needed time to recover. I rested and waited, letting the mud dry so I could kick it off. I soaked in the sun until I felt warm again. I sang low, soft songs until I could breathe again. I looked at flowers, and played in rivers, and dug through the earth for vegetables until I was myself again.

Except that I was not myself. I was something more, something that had become, someone who had grown through those long, dark nights. I thought of my tomato plants, and how they have to be pruned back so much to be strong and healthy, and not everything can grow at once. I thought of my corn, growing tall in the storms, and how weathering so much is what made it so sweet. I thought of my river, and how tears are always "a river that takes you somewhere" (Clarissa Pinkola Estes). This is where I found me, after waiting and pondering, after sitting still and listening, after resting, after being still a very long time, until my spirit was coaxed back to me and my body was ready to breathe again.

It was in the chapels, with sunlight streaming through the stained glass windows, that I reconnected to myself and started living again, even while serving those who were dying. Becoming a chaplain provided a venue for me to give, after so many had served me so well. There were triggers I knew I would face: the deaths of premature infants so small I held their bodies in my palm; the families gathering in the ER to receive the news of loved ones killed in car accidents; and the slow dying of cancer eased only by compassionate palliative care. All of these were harder to face than I thought they would be. The intense personal work involved in rigorous CPE training was good for me, though, both in exposing me to what I had avoided and in the healing that came from letting go of what was already in the past.

I realized that my wounds were already healing, even if they left a mark. Life was moving forward again with every step, for me and the baby I pushed in the stroller. Walking beneath the sky reminded me of how big the world was, and the sunshine thawed me into knowing it was worth the struggle. There was life in the fresh air, and hope in knowing there was more living to do.


When I was diagnosed with ovarian cancer, a caseworker came and picked up two of the children who were living with us, and moved them to a different home. My diagnosis was unexpected and emergent, so she came for the children the same evening we found out about it. Those children were excited to be one step closer to going home, and we all went out to eat to celebrate, but all I could think about was how cancer was robbing me of children once again.

After dinner, we took the children over to Nathan's parents for them to say goodbye. While Nathan kept an eye on the pack, as they rioted through Grandma and Granddad's house, I slipped away with the youngest — a drug baby — for some time to say my farewells in private. It was hard. I cried. But what a gift, to have known her, for even a short bit of time, and maybe helped in some small way we would never know.

What a miracle that, after all those miscarriages, we would get to have our new-parent experiences: bringing a newborn home from the hospital, middle of the night feedings, bottles and burping and diapers galore, and even sleep deprivation! I was so grateful to her, for that little taste of normal, for her sweet smile, and for her tenacity to survive so much in her short life thus far. I cried and I kissed her, I fed her and rocked her one more time, and then I sent her away.

It was strange, after the caseworker loaded up the children and their bags of things and pulled out of the driveway, to come in to an empty and quiet house. My nieces who had come for the summer had already been sent home early, and our teenager that graduated had already moved out on her own. All that was left was Alex and Anber, who had already changed into pajamas and climbed into bed.

I just stood there, listening. Nothing moved. I heard the ticking of a clock for the first time in two years. I started tearing down the streamers and balloons still up in the dining room, left from a foster birthday party. Suddenly they didn't belong anymore, and not just because the birthday was over. It's one thing to be ready to fight cancer, and another thing all together to invite it to a party. There would be no cancer party. So I took the balloons down and threw the whole mess away.

I walked back to the bedroom that was mine and Nathan's before the newborn invasion, and swept it clean of baby stuff. I packed up all the Onesies and zip-up jammies, and moved out the swing and the bouncy seat and the bassinet. I loaded up miniature shoes and gloves and hats, blankets and burp rags. I took empty bottles to the kitchen, and looked for pacifiers the way children look for Easter eggs. I took out the trash, and then cleaned this corner, and then that corner, and then over here, and then over there, and then dusted, and then made Nathan move this and move that, and then vacuumed until I ran out of things to do.

By our third pregnancy, we knew that we were likely to continue miscarrying, and began consciously sharing our pregnancy experiences anyway. The more we shared, the more people came forward in hushed tones and downward glances to talk about their own miscarriages. I had no idea so many people had them, or that it was so not-talked-about. This made us want to talk about it more, not to be a nuisance, but to break the stigma and shake off the shame, especially when we, ourselves, really believe those mighty spirits are still very real and just needed their little bodies.

As it became clear we were not going to carry full-term, we made a conscious decision to celebrate our children in the ways we were able, including giving Nathan's parents a surprise party to announce one of the pregnancies. Getting to do that at least once was really important to us. I am still glad we did, even though that pregnancy also ended in miscarriage after making it seventeen weeks. That celebration is such a good memory, and I needed it because the memory couldn't be stolen from me the way the child was. That's what miscarriage feels like: someone stealing something from you.

I was promised motherhood in my patriarchal blessing, with a "multiplicity of blessings", and I have kissed every cheek and clipped every toenail and put band-aids on every knee and fed all those mouths and tucked in all those babies and prayed with them on my knees on so many nights. I have gone to the courts and heard their stories, driven them to visits that caused them to be mean to me, and cried with them when their parents failed them. I have sent them to time out, given them time-ins, forced them into fake apologetic hugs with their foster siblings, and given my own apologies when it was me who failed. I have worked long hours to clothe them, and used all my PTO taking them for well-child visits and speech therapy and new hearing aid molds. I have celebrated with those whose parents conquered mountains of paperwork arrayed against them, finished classes, cleaned their homes, and welcomed their children into their arms once again. I have driven them to preschool, made hot chocolate for cold mornings waiting on the front porch for junior high buses, and jumped through impossible hoops to get a nearly-grown child her own green card. We have watched a foster teenager grow up, move out, and make us foster-grandparents.

I was never able to carry a child full-term, but I have five times brought babies home from the hospital. I never gave birth from my own body, but I slept with one of our foster babies at the hospital for weeks before she was able to come home with us. I did not get to raise my own biological children during mortality, but my house has been full with more than seventy children in only three years. There are many experiences of motherhood that I have gotten to have because of fostering, and I am grateful for that. I really am, though I know the foster children are not replacements for my own lost babies, any more than I am a replacement mother for their real mothers working so hard to get them home again.

This was my experience: to be pregnant for almost two years solid, and not get to keep any of those babies. This was my experience: to get diagnosed with cancer, and because of nothing I did wrong, caseworkers entered my home and took away the first baby I ever brought home from the hospital, like it was no big deal. This was my experience: to go to the doctor for pain in my hands, get admitted to the hospital for surgery, and wake up without a womb and my vagina sewed closed.

So, we had already been initiated into the Secret Society of Miscarriages, and signed ourselves up for the Benevolent and Parental Order of Fostering. Now was my opportunity to join the world's least popular sorority: Betcha Tākmei Ovum.

I only found out I had ovarian cancer because of the pain in my hands. I was struggling to open baby bottles, but I assumed I was just overly tired. Nathan made me go see the doctor, though, and while I was there and getting blood drawn anyway, I had my annual CA-125 — which had skyrocketed since the year before. My doctor sent me directly over to the gynecologist to see what was happening.

I wanted to cry, sitting there all alone in that waiting room. The office was cold, the walls stark except for baby photography, as if most people go there to have babies instead of lose them. I had tried hard to come to terms with my miscarriages, but on that day my coping skills were already used up, and hot tears stung my eyes despite my best efforts at wearing my brave pants. My bones hurt, and I was so tired that I almost couldn't stay awake just to sit there and wait. *How hard is waiting?* It felt like a blanket of bricks on me, so heavy.

When the nurse finally called my name, I didn't hear her. I had lost myself somewhere between dreaming and crying, but not really breathing. I knew what was coming. I knew, not because I was afraid, but because I had a sense of peace. It was a familiar peace given to me before, the kind that said this was going to be really hard, but everything was going to be okay. The nurse came to me, and touched my shoulder, but my eyes betrayed me, and I wiped my tears before standing. She nodded a smile, as if she already knew, too. She didn't shame me, though, or fake cheerfulness, and I was grateful. She just let me be.

I followed her, though, and did as I was told. I removed my modest Mormon clothes in exchange for a half-gown that covered nothing but my shoulders. I sat, idly swinging my feet in the air, as if I were on the porch swing with Nathan at his parents' house, rather than a doctor's office waiting my turn to be invaded. I stared out the window, watching the tops of trees blow in the wind, imagining that's how my spirit looked as it fought to stay in this mess of a body. I felt my mother there, and my father, too, which startled me at first, but was also a comfort — not just to have them there, but to have them there together. "We have been through this," they said. "We will get you through this," they said. *Why are my tears so hot?* They were such hot tears.

My doctor came back in to talk to me. It felt far away. I heard him discuss my case history, all the people in my family who had died from cancer, the pain I was having, the weird results from my lab work, and my past ultrasounds and scans. It was too much to process, and there was nothing I could do about it, so I just kept looking past him back at the trees. I pretended the branches moved at my breath, and I tried to keep breathing.

"This really does not look good," he said.

"We need to do another ultrasound today," he said.

"Wrap yourself up in a toga here, and walk with us down the hall," he said. Sigh. There is nothing pretty about cancer. There is no place not invaded, no piece of me not looked at by everyone.

My pile of Mormon clothes was left behind, abandoned, as I walked down the hall half-wrapped in a sheet. The regular exam was bad enough, but the trans-vaginal ultrasound was not pleasant, even painful. I was grateful the doctor was so gentle and careful, but he could not make it comfortable. One side hurt worse than the other side. *How long have I hurt this much, and just ignored it?*

"We need to talk," he said. I looked at him then, maybe for the first time, right in the eyes. They were dark and I could see into his soul. He had a mother, and a wife, and a daughter. He looked at me as if I were a daughter, though he knew my parents had both passed already. *So whose daughter am I now?* His eyes were sad and heavy. I wanted to know more, but looked away from him before he saw into mine. I didn't wait for the news.

"Promise me you will be my doctor," I said.

"I will do the surgery," he said, and that's how the conversation started without either of us saying it out loud.

I didn't let him talk until all my Mormon layers were back on, until I could wear my clothes like armor, until I had breathed in the trees and could do the conversation without crying.

"There are at least three large tumors," he said.

"We hope they are benign," he said. "But we won't know until we can get in there and test them."

"But here," he continued, showing me my black and white ultrasound, "here is an even bigger tumor, and this texture and shape indicates it is probably malignant."

I looked back to the trees. I didn't brush away my hot tears any more. For the first time, after all the crying I had done since getting baptized, I didn't wipe them away. They fell freely, and I left them there on my cheek where they fell.

"We won't know for sure until we get in there to look and can do some more scans and some more testing," he went on, "but we need to take everything out as soon as possible." He went on to talk about chemo options, recovery times, and hormone replacement options. It was a blur to me, and the hot tears stung my eyes until I couldn't see the trees. He quietly asked if I had any questions, and handed me a tissue. *What's going to happen to my children? The ones that aren't even mine yet?*

Then, like a slap across my face, he says it's good I have already crossed the bridge about not having children. I can't figure out what bridge he is talking about, or when I crossed it. "It will help," he says. *Help what? How?* I had never consciously decided not to have children. They just weren't born alive. There was no bridge, and I was not willing to cross it.

"Oh, good," I said, not wanting any more discussion, and firmly closing the conversation.

He sent me out, then, with a slow handshake that said "I hope you are still alive next month," simultaneously with "my receptionist will schedule your pre-op".

I got my pre-op appointment card at the front desk, as if it was an invitation to a child's birthday party. The lady tried not to look at me with pity, but was smart enough not to say anything about being excited to see me next time. I told her I would need an interpreter for surgery day, and she promised to take care of it, though experience had taught me not to believe her.

Later, at home in the quiet house after the sibling pair had been taken, I told Nathan that maybe I had to go through this without my mom because she went through hers without me. Maybe it was because of my life before I was baptized. Maybe it was all my fault, and part of the repentance process required of me.

Nathan said, "You have confused God with O. Henry, I think."

He made me laugh, always. With that, we returned to normal, reading our scriptures together and saying our prayers. We didn't worry about whether cancer was stage two or three, or what kind of chemo would let me work the most, or how on earth we would keep me on bed rest for that long. We just smiled, and wrote, and prayed.

That was our summer, the year before Kyrie was born. We enjoyed having only Alex and Anber in the house, a test-run as an all-American nuclear family. For once, there were no just-for-now brothers and sisters coming and going. Our attention and affection were lavished on two, rather than divided between so many, with an over-large share demanded by traumatized newcomers. It looked like a domestic golden age, as long as you squinted your eyes and stepped back from the context.

I made sure to take myself to the community pool one last time before surgery, knowing water to be one of my sacred spaces and that I would miss the rest of summer because of surgery. As families began to head home for dinner, leaving the pool empty, I slowly walked into the water. I could not swim like usual, but my pain was eased as the water buoyed me up, so I slipped under the rope to the deep end.

Keeping my hands in a Namaste position, I kicked my feet like never before, treading water with only my legs moving, kicking until my body remembered I was still alive, until my body remembered I was a fighter, until my body was re-engaged with my spirit and was warmed up for some teamwork.

That's when I choreographed my own interpretive dance, right there in the water. I made myself very still, floating until I felt all the courage and peace I could find inside me. Then I spread my arms out to the sky, thanking the sunshine, thanking Heavenly Parents, and thanking my body. I bowed prostrate under water to my Savior, and swam back up, lifted by the Spirit, feeling the thinness of the veil in the water itself. I reached out my arms to hug my mother, then my father, then my grandparents. Then I stood, straight and tall, and fell backwards under the water, playing baptism like my brother and I did when we were little.

I raised my arms, slowly because they hurt, and touched the scars on my head, and told my body that I was sorry surgery had been so brutal, and that it might be again. I tried to find every scar, every wound, every battle-already-fought and apologized with deep gratitude. I swam for just a minute with my arms only, not long enough to hurt me but long enough to remind me that pain is not the end of things.

Then I took off in an upside down butterfly, doing abdominal crunches up out of the water and then pushing back under. When my belly complained of tumors in the way, I promised to be rid of them soon, but begged to be able to enjoy these last bits of movement before it would all be taken away and I would be cut in pieces, now, while I was still free. *We will have months to rest, my belly and me, but today is our day to move and to play and to breathe.*

I would probably pay for my exuberance with pain the next day, but tomorrow was going to be bad anyway. This was my last day of summer.

I swam and I circled. I did dolphins and tea parties. I swam at the top, and I swam at the bottom. I jumped and leaped and flipped. I danced like a ballerina, and I swam like an Emily. It was in three acts, my dance, because I had to take a lot of naps. When I finished, and took my bow, my parents clapped for me. *Brava!* I bowed again, and not caring who could see, caring only who I could see. I collapsed in my chair, too far gone, needing another nap before I could gather my things and my Self and head back home. It didn't matter how much I had done, or had dreamed, or had only imagined. It only mattered that the wind began to blow, and I began to laugh. Because I knew I'd done it. I had danced up a storm.

I hadn't picked a fight with cancer. It picked a fight with me. And so a fight was what it was gonna get.

When I woke from surgery, we anxiously awaited news on the biopsy. The surgeon surprised us when he said that he had never seen anything like what he had found in me. Even the oncologist had only seen it discussed at a conference once. That was why surgery took five hours instead of forty-five minutes. There were, as he suspected from the ultrasounds and scans, three smaller non-malignant tumors the size of baseballs, and one larger malignant tumor a little smaller than a basketball. What was unique, though, was that instead of it being one of those soft tumors they must pull out so carefully, so as not to break or spill any of the cancer, mine had formed into what looked like hard rocks. Not only that, but the malignant one had spread like a string of pearls, and wrapped around both ovaries and tubes, pulling them together. It then lassoed around my uterus, cutting it off and pulling it back where it had attached as a tangled mess to my pelvic bone and lower spine.

Before surgery, I had sought priesthood blessings once again, and they had contained words that had seemed incomprehensible: the cancer cells were commanded to organize themselves, because they were out of order, even for cancer. I couldn't help but remember those words now, as the doctor talked about how my cancer had organized itself into these rocky chains. He said that, while it was a bizarre presentation of cancer, it probably saved my life. If the cancer had not grown and spread in that unique way, it would have already spread to my liver and lungs.

I had thought that resting and being still would be hard for me, like after other surgeries, but this time, cancer and anemia and low blood counts wiped me out. I was grateful for any moments with my eyes open. It was the first time words were lost to me, as I couldn't stay awake enough to think clearly and had too much pain to type. That would be the hardest part for me over the next two years: not being able to write.

Nathan was amazing during my hospital stay, caring for the children all day until putting them to bed. Once they were asleep, his parents would come over to sit with them while Nathan came back to be with me at the hospital. It would be late enough that the doors would be locked, and he would have to wind his way through to me from the ER entrance. He was so strong, and so faithful, and so good to me, even on those days with very little comfort or rest or sleep. He is my best friend for a reason, you know, and I grew to love him more than ever.

There in my hospital room, we read our scriptures together, and prayed. He put lotion on my skin, and sang me a lullaby while I cried at the pain just from moving my body enough to lie back down. I did have moments without pain, but getting up and down stabbed my incisions with a thousand daggers.

He was patient and careful with me, my Nathan, and every tear he wiped away further endeared him to me. I was not afraid when he was near, and knew that whether this battle was one year or fifty, he would always be my favorite part of mortality and worth every bit of it. Our eternity had begun long ago, and he had always been a part of my plan of happiness.


I slept in my faux silk pajamas, and when I woke and stood, I was aware of how they moved with me. They blew in the wind of the fans that kept me cool, went with me when I had the energy to stand. Until I was ready for my shower, and then my pajamas were tossed aside. *Is that what I would look like — not me, just my mortal self — when my time here was done?*

I had always thought dying would be like slipping into a pool, something warm and inviting. I thought it would be a relief, after the pains and struggles of mortality. I thought the water released you, lifting from you the heavy burdens of gravity. I thought it was a jumping in and sinking down until touching bottom, then being catapulted up toward the light, faster and faster until you can finally fly. That is part of it, but only part. There is also the setting aside.

I know that when I die, it will be because I have been called to serve my parents, to finish duking it out with them, to joyfully be reunited with them, to be forgiven and embraced by them. When I die, it will not be because of cancer. It will be because I finally got my call, the envelope I have been waiting on, legitimately assigned to go serve my parents and finish what we started here.

Cancer is not my fault, and is not a consequence of some past sin. But it does make sense to me, in my context, why this would be a battleground I must cross. So for the moment, I continue to choose mortality. Even with its pain and loss, I choose mortality because Nathan is here, and the children are here, and there is work to do.

I choose the husband I prayed for since I was a child. I choose the five-year-old redhead whom I asked if he bit his lip and he said, "No, mama! I hit it on Nicholas's head!" I choose the little brown four-year-old who is finally beginning to attach and to trust. As the years of my cancer battle continued, my choice became also for Mary, and then Kirk and Barrett, and then Kyrie — even when she was born with more hair than I had after chemo.

Living meant keeping my spirit strong. It meant praying before eating my food, even though I wouldn't be able to finish it. It meant reading my scriptures every morning, even though I might fall asleep. It meant looking pain in the face, and breathing my way through the rhythm of it.

I was in the hospital for a week before I could go home. I wasn't strong yet, or able to lift Anber or carry Alex around on my back. But my incision was healing, and my organs had all been re-stitched to grow back into the places they should have been in the first place. With more time, I would be able to sit, and maybe even to get in and out of bed. No one would feel like clapping just because I had a bowel movement, or cheer when I woke up from a nap without a fever, but these achievements were markers of my recovery.

People know the chemo story all survivors must endure, and I was famous for celebrating ovarian cancer with my fantastic teal wig. But the deeper battle I conquered was learning to care for myself. I could no longer push myself as I had before cancer, and could no longer live at such an insane pace — working full time with six children at home, with a part-time job at the ER, while in two post-doc programs, and also simultaneously doing CPE units at two different hospitals more than an hour away from home. I learned to limit extra work projects, to say no when I was ill or in pain, and to protect resting days with fierce determination. When my body required naps, I succumbed without complaint. I learned to juice, took walks instead of running, and gained the weight from medications and hormones as gracefully as I could. I was all together a different person physically, and seemed to grow very old over the course of just one summer.

Sometimes my body could not fight another moment, and collapsed into fever-sleep. It was tempting to just let go, because my parents were already there, on the other side of the veil, and because I was so trapped in my body here but could be so busy there, with that light that was so very bright. I would struggle to wake again, and felt my spirit yearning to fly away.

I knew I wasn't dying yet, but I also was aware my condition was precarious for a time. It wasn't that my body had quit or was giving up, so much as it was that my spirit had gone away to class. There were Heavenly things for me to see, and spiritual things for me to ponder. There were assignments for me to receive, and skills for me to learn. I was grateful for the times when sleep or the nourishment and distraction of friends buoyed me up through the water and made time pass more quickly during that dreadful illness, truly. But I also had an internal understanding that some of my most powerful lessons come from those moments where spiritual eons pass during a single moment of physical pain.

This, I think, is some of the power that Kyrie holds. She has learned those same lessons in less than a year of mortality, and all those who meet her can feel her spirit testify of heavenly things. The timing in which she entered our lives confirmed her as a tender mercy, and there was something eternal that glued us together as we fought to survive, she and I. Mary said it best on the phone that day, as I walked with Kyrie through mists of water that cooled us on that hot day at the zoo: "Mama keeps the baby alive, and the baby keeps Mama alive."

# 13

There is only one thing in the world worse than turning the pins on your baby's jaw distractor to break her little face and make the bones grow. Once the distractors were out, twice a day I had to take special antibiotic ointment and push down hard on those little wounds to rub in the medicine. It's called "aggressive scar massage," and it was torture for both of us. But once again, the doctors and nurses knew what they were talking about — it helped minimize scarring of the tissue where the pins had been. I hated hurting her, but we worked hard at it for the rest of the year, so that when spring came, her scars were barely noticeable even by touch.

Other scars were less noticeable, though, and not exclusive to Kyrie: the emotional scars from early childhood trauma. The last thing our other children needed was for me to disappear for six weeks. After all they had endured, from abandonment to serial foster placements, and with the formation of our own family still so new, it was a traumatic thing for me to be sent away. They understood in their heads, as much as they could at those young ages, that I was in Cincinnati with the baby and had not disappeared intentionally or permanently. But, in effect, I was one more mother who had left them.

217

Staying in contact with the children was critical during those months I was away. Nathan and I let them call on video phone, and I let them talk with Kyrie every day that she was well enough. That way, she could continue bonding with the pack of children who would be her brothers and sisters, while they were so eager to see our faces. I used FaceTime to take them on tours of the hospital, and RMHC, and even the zoo. I sent them pictures of the food I ate, the stickers we used to decorate the tapes on Kyrie's face, and me posing with the Ronald McDonald statue on the bench outside RMHC.

Summer is a busy birthday season in our family, and while Kyrie and I were in Cincinnati, we missed three: Anber's, Mary's, and Nathan's. It felt like yet another tragedy, after all the hard work of attachment we had done. We handled it the best way we could, with a small party on their special days that I could attend by video, with the promise of a big celebration once we were all back together. I got to sing "Happy Birthday" to each one, and sent special gifts home from the craft room at RMHC, but it just wasn't the same.

There were several reasons we were separated for so long, but the biggest was that we never actually knew how long we were going to be there. We were first told it would be just a week, and then it was another week to get the distractors on. The plan was to send us home while the distractors were being turned, and then to come back after a month or two to have them removed. However, when Kyrie remained in a coma after surgery, and then had so many crises requiring re-hospitalization after that, we never were released to go home. We had not expected that we would end up being gone so long, but it just happened a day at a time.

Several families in our ward and community offered to help get Nathan and the children up to see us, and I was so grateful for their generosity. I could picture no greater relief than being able to hold them all in my arms. However, we didn't yet know anyone they could stay with, and could not afford a hotel for the family for an unknown length of time. I had my room with the baby at RMHC, but we were a family of eight, and RMHC rooms can only hold four people. Eventually, we decided it was important enough to at least have Nathan come for a short visit, maybe even to trade places so that we could each get a change of pace in our single parenting. But by the time we settled on that idea, Kyrie was finally ready to be discharged and coming home anyway.

The children are still anxious now, anytime Kyrie has to be back in the hospital. We make sure to help them feel safe and included in any way we can. When she is hospitalized locally, they come visit her. When she has to travel out of state for the hospital, we work to raise the money to do it as a family. We also encourage people to donate the funds to RMHC for a few bigger rooms that could host families with more than two children.

I knew that one day, when we would return to Cincinnati, I would be sure to share with the children as much of my Cincinnati experience as I could. I would make sure they got an official tour, seeing everything I had shown them in video and pictures — especially the RMHC playground, which really excited them. I imagined cooking a meal together in the kitchen, and eating together on the patio. I knew it would be a necessary ritual for our family, an experience to bring healing to wounds still open from the summer before.

We traveled a surprising amount with our foster children. We took monthly drives to the LDS temple in Oklahoma City, as well as journeys to Mormon historical church sites like Kansas City, Nauvoo, Kirtland, and Salt Lake City. Weekends in Branson, Missouri became almost a rite of passage for new arrivals. We found that these trips not only provided a positive bonding opportunity, and exposed to the children to new experiences, but also the process of going away and coming back to our home had a settling effect, as if helping the children to really believe they were in a place they could trust. Silver Dollar City was often a highlight of those trips, with its roller coasters and carousels tucked in between country bands and old-timey artisan workshops.

One time we were leaving Silver Dollar City on the parking lot shuttle, the same as we had ridden many times before, except this time Anber was finally old enough to have enjoyed the park so much that she didn't want to leave. She began screaming before we got to the stop near our van, and by the time we got off the shuttle she was biting me and kicking me and screaming at me. I moved her under some shade for a two-minute time out, but she wriggled away and took off running and screaming across the parking lot. I chased after her, waving cars out of the way, and people stared as if I were kidnapping her.

I brought her back to the time out spot, and sat next to her as she screamed. Strangers walking by offered her popcorn and candy to make her feel better, and it made me crazy. I was trying to extinguish a behavior, not reinforce it. But she wasn't even being naughty, really; she was trying to meet her needs for safety and provision and comfort in the only way she knew how. My aim was to teach her how to do that in more pro-social ways than biting, kicking, or screaming.

I knew it was even bigger than just a parking lot meltdown. When drug babies grow up to be children who crave adrenaline and cortisol and dopamine, it is easy for them to turn into adolescents who self-medicate with drugs. This wasn't just about stopping a temper tantrum; it was about saving an addict.

Addiction involves craving something intensely, loss of control over its use, and continuing involvement with it despite adverse consequences. The adverse consequence in that moment was duking it out with Mama in the gravel. When she is a teenager, the adverse consequences could be diseases and neurological damage or death. It seemed to me, despite the circus show in public, that it was better to intervene and start wrestling through this while she was still young.

Addiction changes the brain, first by subverting the way it registers pleasure and then by corrupting other normal drives, such as learning and motivation. It was a Helen Keller v. Annie Sullivan cage match, because Anber's brain had been changed by drug exposure in utero and as an infant. The time out (which really was a "time in" with me there next to her) was a part of her healing, rather than punitive.

Being consistent without compelling, and attentive without smothering, was exhausting. But finally, Anber began to calm. When her screaming began to slow, I said a prayer and patted her back and counted with her as she started breathing again. We stayed there and sang soft songs while the cortisol and adrenaline finished pumping out of her system, because when she gets that worked up, she literally cannot calm herself down.

Finally, that worn-out child, sweaty from battle, collapsed into me and began to cry instead of scream, and then just grew quiet, and then finally let me rub her back. "I am sorry for screaming, Mama." I held her hand as we walked back to the van, picking up her shoes and everything else she had thrown across the parking lot while she was screaming. I was not being mean, but teaching her that her choices have consequences, and the consequences are hers to clean up.

She apologized to Nathan, too, and to the other children, who knew to give her space as she collected herself and caught her breath. After she was safely buckled in her seat, Nathan and I connected behind the van with a hug as we debriefed.

We so want our children to be successful and happy and well. Despite what it looks like in those kinds of moments, all of our children are actually surprisingly obedient (except for when they are not). Their fits are not about defiance; they are about safety and attachment. When Kyrie cries, it means she is hungry or cold or needs to be changed. Because she has been with us her whole life, she has healthy attachment to us, and knows we will meet her needs. The crying and screaming from our other children is altogether different, because they are still learning to trust that we will keep them safe, and that we will still be there when they wake after nap time.

But when they are functioning well, and know what is expected of them, they are very good at doing what is asked. In fact, sometimes they are overly compliant, because they think it keeps them safe. Earlier in that same day at Silver Dollar City, when we had to put the three babies down for a nap in the middle of the theme park, I found a shady spot and laid down blankets. I didn't even have to tell Anber what to do. She hopped out of her seat in the stroller, laid down, and snuggled into the spot where she would sleep. What two-year-old does that? I got down with her, right in front of everybody, and talked softly to her while I took off her shoes. I adjusted her little head to a softer place on the blanket. I tucked her in a little. I patted her back and sang a song. I did the tiny things she doesn't really need, or even know she that she wants, because that is good touch, and because that is attachment building.

Early intervention is critical with these children. The years Mary missed by not hearing anything or having any access to sign language, were not just about ABC's and learning her numbers; they were significant years of incidental learning that cannot be taught. The time lost from Kirk not being taken to neurologist appointments or missing physical therapy sessions is the time it took for his left arm to grow limp and sleepy, when it had been weak but still awake and full of potential. For Kyrie, our urgency was not just a battle for air, but a fight for her brain and her development;

we had already seen firsthand what happens when little ones with challenges are neglected.

In Oklahoma, the early intervention team is called SoonerStart, and consists of speech-pathology, physical, occupational, and developmental therapists. This team saw her weekly or twice weekly anytime she wasn't in the hospital, and several times came to work with her when she was admitted. More times than we could count, they worked with her extra, without reimbursement, because they knew she was in crisis and needed more help.

This team of ladies was with us on the front line, battling to save our children. They helped Kyrie deal with developmental regression after hospital stays, and tracked how long after a surgery or illness it took her to get back to her baseline. They witnessed her sudden and severe desats, and the extreme lethargy when she was off oxygen or when she was sick — symptoms that had been frustratingly invisible during hospital observation. Knowing where her development should be, and knowing Kyrie so intimately, they were the ones who wouldn't let us accept this level of "normal", and who helped us push Kyrie beyond her expected limitations.

We also had nutritionist and dietitian consults from Cincinnati, who confirmed that Kyrie's small size was not due to a low caloric intake. Despite high calorie formula, plus adding fats and oils to her table food, she was gaining weight too slowly and would drop weight dramatically any time we took her off oxygen or she got sick. We were grateful that, after being on and off the NG tube so many times during her first year, she had no food or texture aversions. That girl loved to eat, but she also needed air to grow.

Together, these teams helped us advocate for the help Kyrie needed. They gave us resources, and found us contact information, and communicated with other members of her healthcare team. They were the ones who helped us navigate all the doctor drama, whether it was her local pediatrician and nurse practitioner that we loved, or the team of half a dozen specialists across the country. If it were not for the early intervention team, Kyrie would still be unable to move her left side, or worse: we firmly believe that Kyrie would not have survived the first year without the good care and attention they gave her.

They helped refer us for help with issues not as critical as breathing, but still crucial for Kyrie's development. She had to see the eye doctor because her left eye was "stuck" in the wrong place and not responsive; the eye doctor said it was cerebral palsy affecting the fourth nerve of her eye, and he asked why she wasn't trached. She saw the audiologist, because she kept failing hearing tests until she got tubes in her ears, and we were relieved to know her hearing was improving. She got braces for her tiny feet, while the therapists said Kyrie just was not going to use them much or be very active until she got her trach, and why hadn't that happened yet? We had the same questions ourselves.

All these appointments were hard work, though, and meant our schedule was filled with therapists instead of soccer games. There were multiple appointments with the early intervention team, a neurologist, a pulmonologist, an audiologist, a pediatric ophthalmologist, a local ENT, an ENT specialist in Utah, plus the team in Cincinnati. Besides that, the other children needed their helper teams as well: Mary saw an audiologist for cochlear implant mappings, plus a speech therapist every week; Alex needed autism services and physical therapy; Kirk saw a neurologist and was in physical therapy; and all of the children were in counseling, as well. There were also IEP teams at school for each child, where similar services were provided in smaller time frames (because that's how much Oklahoma prioritizes schools in the state budget). That doesn't even include well-child checks, eye exams, and dental visits that all six children needed. There were also monthly visits by each child's caseworker, quarterly home inspections, and visits with biological parents — which could be as often as every week per child, and even requiring us to transport the child to other cities. We at one time had 37 appointments in our home every week just for all the help the children needed to function and grow to their potential. We were busy!

About a month after her first birthday, Kyrie started sleeping more and more. When she was awake, she played sitting down and stopped running after the other children. By the time she was fourteen months old, she had been sleeping about twenty hours a day for five weeks. We told this to the pulmonologist, who said to give her another nebulizer treatment to ensure her lungs were functioning as well as they could.

The doctors had instructed us to leave her off oxygen as much as possible. She could hold her sats in the 80s and 90s, but she was very fussy, eating only when we woke her for food, and no longer participating in any gross motor activities.    Even in her physical or developmental therapy sessions, they had to stop working on kicking and running and climbing, and instead she played with flashcards of animals and the names of body parts.   Even then, after about twenty minutes, she would just roll to the ground panting, and stay there.

The scariest piece of this, though, was when she quit trying.

She completely stopped playing, and started stumbling and falling when she tried to walk. Instead of her toddler nap routine, she was sleeping twenty hours a day or more.   For the first time, her color changes when she had a desat were more often central than only peripheral, giving her blue lips instead of only blue hands. Then she stopped eating, for four days, for the first time in her life — even as a newborn, when she struggled so much to keep her formula down, she never stopped trying.    Her weight dropped from sixteen pounds to just under fourteen pounds.

The light was gone from her eyes, as if she had no strength to fight.  During one developmental therapy session, she covered her eyes and then passed out; when we roused her, she crawled over to her oxygen concentrator and signed "more please" as she fell down crying.    Desperate to help her and not receiving additional guidance from the specialists, our nurse practitioner sent us to the ER.

The staff at our local hospital gave her fluids by IV, but were not prepared to deal with such a fragile airway. When they said she needed an NG tube but were reluctant to put it in her, I told them I could do it myself. Using my training from Cincinnati, I measured the long yellow tube from her nose to her ear, and then from her ear to under her rib cage. I slipped one end up her nose, and in rhythm with her cries, gently pushed it in using her swallows to help it go down. The ER team did an X-ray for me to confirm placement, and I had nailed it.

Following up on this incident, the pulmonologist called us to his office. What we needed was an ENT, who would be able to look at the structural challenges of Kyrie's PRS airway. Instead, Medicaid referred her to a pulmonologist, whose specialty is the lungs. It sounds like a minor difference, but the consequences have been enormous, and the red tape surrounding any change has been impenetrable.

The pulmonologist told us that he had spoken with the ENT in Utah, and agreed that it sounded like it was finally time for a trach. *Good news!* He said Kyrie would be admitted to the hospital right away. *Thank you!* But then he started to talk about breathing, and how three things contribute to it: the lungs, which take in air, and the heart, which pumps oxygen throughout the body, and the brain, which tells the lungs to do their job. If she wasn't getting enough air, it was because of one of these things, he said.

We told him that her physical therapist talked about how her chest cavity was too short and too small, how her shoulders were hunched up from trying so hard to breathe, and how the muscles on her back were too tight from not being used. We told him about her passing out, and sleeping too much, and not having energy to play. However, he could only see that her lungs were fine, though still needing to grow. He wanted to rule out heart or brain issues before traching her, ignoring the constricted airway that was the core of the problem (which a trach would bypass).

Please understand: her pulmonologists have been some of the kindest, most pleasant doctors we have worked with, doting on Kyrie and always returning our emergency calls quickly. They are doing their best, and they are good doctors. The problem has been, with almost all of our doctors, that looking at Kyrie through the blinders of their own medical specialties has prevented them from communicating with each other or seeing the whole child.

Kyrie underwent heart testing because she had a history of heart murmur, as well as a small hole in her heart, a common occurrence with PRS babies because of the mid-line development issues. The echo cardiogram showed that the hole had closed, and gave no evidence of a heart murmur. There was some hypertension from working too hard to breathe, but nothing that overly concerned them.

He also ordered that Kyrie be hooked up for twenty-four hours to an EEG, monitoring brain waves to see if she was having seizures. She wasn't. He also ruled out any impact on breathing from the stroke she had had following one of her early surgeries.

Since all of these tests came back negative, and because she maintained sats the whole time, the pulmonologist concluded that she was not in crisis, and took traching her off the table again. Of course, their tests didn't reveal anything about her behavioral and developmental delays, nor her repeated weight losses. There wasn't even any comment on the fact that a fourteen-month-old toddler was stuck in a crib for twenty-four hours — and she just sat there contentedly. The doctors were missing the obvious while they were so focused on the numbers: there was a serious gap between what the monitors showed and the complex reality of what was going on.

Doctors may need numbers for evidence-based research, but ethically they are responsible to look at all the data, including behavioral and developmental data (which can also be quantified if that's what they need). We were concerned about this, after having been told so many times by so many different professionals that Kyrie was compensating for her acceptable sats by not moving, and using up all her caloric energy on trying to breathe. We had been asked by so many why she had not been trached yet, and were warned that jaw distraction was not always sufficient in preventing secondary complications regardless of sat and sleep study numbers.

The first children to have endured jaw distraction are only now becoming adults, and many of them have suffered from behavioral challenges and psychoses because of ongoing hypoxemia, which means not enough oxygen in the brain. There is no way to predict exactly what Kyrie's long-term consequences will be, but her continued cyanosis, or the dusky dark color of her hands and feet, means that her organs are not getting enough oxygen to function well. Avoiding a trach by fancy plastic surgery doesn't count as the least restrictive level of care if it keeps her brain prisoner, trapped and struggling for enough air to stay alive, no matter what the monitors say.

After the pulmonologist discharged Kyrie, without her even being looked at by an ENT, the nurses and techs came in to remove the sensors, to detach her monitors, and to take out her IV. We could finally take her out of the crib and hold her after twenty-four hours of confinement. We cleaned her up, starting the awful process of getting glue out of her hair once again, and got her lotioned and dressed. Nathan put her down on the ground, and she happily took off running out the door to explore. She slowed before she got to the nurse's desk, however, and then her strength failed her, and she toppled over. Not willing to give up, she started crawling, but even that was too much for her, and she soon came to a stop and just sat there panting. That's not a healthy toddler. Regardless of numbers, our baby still could not breathe *enough*, and we knew by then that neither Cincinnati nor Oklahoma was going to trach her, and Medicaid would not pay for another full workup in Utah.

We felt resigned to following the orders of the doctors, letting her baseline just be her baseline, no matter how much we worried. Maybe our vision had been clouded by some kind of parental-medical-PTSD, but it felt like defeat, settling for what we had told everyone was unacceptable. Her early intervention team still thought that a trach would allow her gross motor skills to catch up, and remove any need for feeding tubes. But they are not the doctors, and couldn't make it happen for her. Nathan and I are still convinced that if Kyrie had been trached early on, she would not have needed repeated hospitalizations, or have had the struggles she has endured — including a stroke, a coma, and medical cerebral palsy.

We fought hard, we fought for a whole year, but now she had passed her first birthday. It was a milestone marked by a crowd of Kyrie fans, from extended family to Facebook friends, who crowded into our home one Sunday afternoon to honor this little miracle child. Everyone says that PRS babies get better after a year, because they finally start to grow and get stronger. Maybe her year mark was just coming a little late because she was born early, or from drug baby delays. Or maybe we had been in denial, and just caused a whole lot of problems by fighting for what we couldn't really change. We aren't doctors, and we don't know anything, and we have been confused by so many people with so many ideas, and every hospital having a different philosophy of care.

Kyrie has good doctors. She really does. We love them. They are kind and patient. They think we are crazy because we have not stopped pestering them for help, but they love her and take good care of her. They cannot change the fact that she wasn't trached a year ago any more than we can, but what we can do is work together to take care of her now.

She will continue to battle consequences from the last year, but the time to intervene to prevent them has passed. So we will let her be, and do our best with what we have learned. She will not be pink, and she will always be happier on the days when she had oxygen the night before. But she has two brown sisters, so being a little dusky will help her blend in. And she is alive. That's the most important thing.

I think what hurt the most was that we were not able to stop Kyrie from being "damaged" by the life she had before us. I think that, up until that moment when trach surgery was canceled at the last minute for the third time, I still thought that if we got custody early enough, and advocated hard enough, we could protect her from having to endure the kinds of traumas our other children have been through.

In reality, life is just hard sometimes. We can't undo what already is, and the challenge is moving forward in faith. Sometimes your dad dies of cancer. Sometimes a guy in a Jeep smashes into your mom's car. Sometimes ovarian cancer happens. Sometimes your baby is born not breathing, and red tape and medical politics keep her blue.

Sometimes the mistakes are your own. Could I have been more gentle with Anber when she screamed and hit at me? Why didn't I do another head count before accidentally leaving Alex at home, that time we called the police because we thought he was lost at the park? Wasn't there any way I could have skipped straight past the rebellious years of my young adulthood and started gathering my children before cancer had taken so much out of me?

But this is mortality, and living is how we gain our wisdom. I try my best, hopefully learn from my mistakes, and keep moving forward, one stumble at a time.

# 14

When I opened my eyes at 5:00 a.m., it felt like no time had passed, but I needed to get back to Kyrie. I listened to scriptures as I walked across to the hospital from RMHC, being reminded by those prophetic words that we are not forgotten. I needed to hold on to the idea that God remembers us, that He knows us, and that He loves us. This lifted the exhaustion from me, as I flashed my "support person" badge — because I was not yet a "parent" — to get upstairs, and then made my way through the maze to her room.

I needed to trust in God's unfailing care, because this is how quickly things could change in Cincinnati:

One night, before the distractors had been removed, Kyrie and I were playing on the bed at RMHC. I had her propped up on the Boppy for tummy time, and she was practicing transferring brightly colored links from one hand to the other, when she suddenly coughed so hard that her NG tube flew out of her mouth and slapped me right on the face. It scared her, and startled me! The tube was still in her nose, and the tapes holding it there were perfectly placed, but the end of the tube that was supposed to be in her stomach now hung out of her mouth.

It was the only time that we were not in a rush to get to the ER because it wasn't an actual emergency. It did bother her as it hung off her face, but it wasn't hurting her at all. I needed to get it back in, though, before her next feeding was due. I loaded her stroller with the suctioning machine and diapers, and took us on a walk back across the street to the hospital.

Now familiar with her bright eyes and the feeding tube she didn't want to keep in, the ER team got us back quickly to help me replace it. But when they did the usual check-in process, weighing her and taking her temperature, they discovered she had a fever. We thought maybe it was because she was playing with a blanket on our walk through the summer heat, so we unbundled her and waited for her to cool off before checking her temperature a second time. It went up. Her fever was officially rising, and so she was admitted for the fourth time in six weeks — this time to a regular floor that did not understand about distraction or small airways. Not having planned on her being admitted, I had not brought much with us and had to return to RMHC without her to gather our things.

When I returned, I was surprised to see infectious disease precautions on her door, and everyone in mask and gloves and gowns. I was told she had been given a chest X-ray to check for pneumonia, and that they had drawn blood to see what was causing the fever. Until they had those answers, or all her forty-eight hour cultures come back normal, she was on strict precautions, just in case.

She had seemed to be doing alright, but as the day passed, she clearly grew worse. They couldn't find the infection, so they didn't know how to treat it. She was obviously sick, though, and they couldn't delay treatment — except that once they used antibiotics, the infection would hide, making it even harder to find out what was wrong. They said that, normally, babies younger than six months don't get fevers. That meant an infant with a fever from an infection they could not find was in danger of being consumed by sepsis, which causes organ failure, which causes death. They were working against the clock, while her overworked body was desperately trying to heal itself. She didn't have the immune system to fight very long, everyone told me, because babies just don't. Once again, she was critical, where the next twenty-four hours would tell us if she would live or not.

By night, her fever was even higher. Her pain was out of control. Her secretions grew so thick and dark they clogged the suction machines, and sometimes there was blood. Her condition was deteriorating rapidly, and I sent updates to Nathan while she slept fitfully. We also updated the HousewifeClass.com blog and put out the call: *Pray for this little girl. She needs a miracle; she needs your prayers.* The community response was immense, and we were in awe as her temperature stopped rising and held steady.

By the next morning, her fever had broken. Her lab work was "strangely the same, but not worse," they said. Her secretions were back to normal and clear, and she was managing them again on her own. They couldn't explain what had happened, and all her virus panels came back negative. They had suspected meningitis, but ruled that out as well. They only had two possible explanations: first, drug babies are just unpredictable, and you often can't explain what their bodies do; and second, maybe she aspirated but we got to the ER so fast, and got her antibiotics so quickly, that we actually managed to prevent pneumonia instead of getting it and then needing to treat it. A lot of prayerful people and I could have offered an additional explanation.

That was the reality here, though. Her condition could improve or drop like a roller coaster in the space of a breath. We were blessed by faith and prayers, but in a hospital there are many times when the answer must be no.

Now, after distraction removal, I fought to keep that shadow from my mind as I held this miracle who was mine but not yet mine. She smiled at me, as best she could with her swollen little face. Finally free of the distractors, I saw her tongue for the first time, popped up out of her throat and into place where it should be. She took a big, unobstructed breath, closed her eyes, and slept in peace for the first time ever. As she slept, her heart rate stayed down in the 120's, and her carbon dioxide began to clear, and her oxygen began to rise, and her lips turned red instead of blue. The distraction had worked, and she was breathing. And she was pink!

Once we knew the distraction had done its job, they began working on discharge planning. Pleased with her progress, the case managers connected us with home health back in Oklahoma. That way the baby would have the supplies she needed before we even got home, and we would not have the problems we had when she came home from the hospital the first time.

In the days that followed, she even began chewing on her hand, which was the first sign of her starting to stimulate that new mouth! It meant we got to re-introduce the pacifier, because it would help shape and align her mouth correctly. That's one more step toward eating by mouth instead of the NG tube. I was so proud of her, and so grateful for her dramatic improvement.

She was a happy baby, smiling and starting to giggle, and those smiles lit up my whole being. The one drama we had was caring for her face. She hated it. The places where the metal bars had gone through her bones were still tender. But, as I had been instructed, I pushed and rubbed on her exact sore places so that even her scars could heal. It made her cry, and it made me cry, and I wondered if that is what God feels like sometimes when he pushes me through hard things so that I can more fully heal.

When it was just us, she was "talking" to me all the time, despite her tongue still sewn to her lip. I kept words going, whether in sign language or my voice. We read scriptures together every morning, and listened to audio books during her feedings. We finished *Winnie the Pooh* and *Treasure Island* and *Jane Eyre*. She cried if I stopped between chapters!

When Kyrie was finally ready to leave the hospital, it was time for me to bring all of her things back to RMHC. It was nearly a disaster. There was so much to do, and I was already exhausted. "It was a farce," I told Nathan, "like one of those old movies full of physical comedy and doors slamming."

Cincinnati's Ronald McDonald House was close enough for me to walk from the hospital, just a block away, but to carry all of Kyrie's equipment on a day when rain was coming down in sheets made the free shuttle a more appealing option. However, the shuttle only came every half hour, so timing was everything.

I had to go to RMHC to meet the NG tube supply person, and so I caught the 10:30 a.m. shuttle to get over there. I waited for twenty minutes for my appointment to arrive, then got a message from her that she needed a picture of the end of Kyrie's NG tube to know which syringes would be compatible. I had to run back to the hospital through the rain, up to the baby's room through three security checkpoints, take a picture, race back down, and make it in time to catch the 11:00 a.m. shuttle back to RMHC.

"Didn't I just drop you off?" the driver asked.

"Forgot something," I explained.

Getting off at RMHC, I ran in to meet the NG tube person. Except because of something-I-didn't-understand-what-she-said-on-the-phone, she was going to be an hour late — which turned into two hours late. While I waited on her, I worked on getting Kyrie's things "home", one wagon load at a time. She had a lot of stuff! There were machines and tubes and equipment and accessories and positioning pillows, plus all the normal baby paraphernalia.

So for two hours, I took a wagon load down from her hospital room, loaded it onto the shuttle, rode over to RMHC, unloaded it off of the shuttle, carried it all upstairs to our second floor room, then ran down and back through the rain and up to her room again for another load.

After finally meeting with the NG tube supplier, I headed back to the hospital to get Kyrie — but the nurse sent me down to the pharmacy to pick up her prescriptions. The pharmacy needed my ID, and my ID was still in my room at RMHC.

Back on the shuttle.

I got my wallet from our room, and ran through the rain back to the hospital. I showed the pharmacy my ID and her foster placement papers (which I had thought to grab), and the pharmacist said her medicine would be ready in two more hours. I went back up to the unit, and was told the I had a meeting with the suction machine supply person back at RMHC.

Yes. Back on the shuttle.

I got back to RMHC just in time for them to call and say the supplier had gone to the hospital instead, so I ran back through the rain and back up to the unit. He had three large boxes of things for me, so I loaded them up in a wagon headed back down to the shuttle. Loaded it on the shuttle, unloaded, up to our room, back through the rain to the hospital.

Just as I arrived, the nurse told me the NG tube supplier was back again, waiting for me at RMHC with more supplies for the weekend, "but everything else will be a big delivery on Tuesday." *How much stuff does a baby need?*

After carrying the weekend supplies up to our room, I was ready, then, to run (a little more slowly) back to the hospital again, get the prescriptions, and *finally* pick up Kyrie, except by then it was after 8:00 p.m., and RMHC recommends its residents do not walk over from the hospital at night. So I had to sit and wait in the foyer of RMHC for the 9:00 p.m. ride back to the hospital. Once they dropped me off, I had a half hour to feed her one more time, change an explosive diaper, take out all her IV's, get her loaded up in the carrier backpack, sign discharge papers, check her out through security, and get back downstairs on time for the final shuttle of the day.

At last, I got Kyrie up to our room at nearly 10:00 p.m., just in time to get her suctioned, give her evening meds, and put her down for the night.    I sat down for a moment, my feet and body exhausted and aching, and realized I had ridden every single shuttle that day, from 10:30 a.m. to 9:30 p.m. It was worth it to have her close, to watch her sleep, to be "home" with her.

As it turns out, Nathan and I are terrible parents! At least it can feel that way. We don't mean to be, and we try hard, but we are not confident in this department. We understand in new ways, after the experiences of the last few years, why families are a required part of the plan of happiness. It's not because they are perpetually happy. Parenting shines light on shadows in your soul that you never even knew were there until some child drags them out of you shrieking and swinging, and what shame and frustration that feels like! Nothing has been so refining, so challenging, or so shocking as our parenting experiences and behaviors.

For years, long before children, I would take an annual retreat in a nearby monastery. It was like an extended Sabbath to me, a Jubilee of sorts, and the silence of those days fueled me for the coming year. But

I am not called to live the monastic lifestyle that now seems so dream-like and far away. I am not called to leave my home, to be free to play in academics, or to journey at will. Life moves in seasons, and my time for that may come again. But for now, I am called to serve Nathan, to care for children, and to work on my home (temporally and spiritually) until it is a temple space. We have a long way to go for that, but we are trying.

I know some will frown at us for taking on so many children so quickly, and some do not believe we are organized enough to provide positive attention, time-ins, and healthy interactions with each child individually. Some will roll their eyes when a toddler's potty emergency makes us late for church again, or when I put a screaming child in time out in a public place. I don't claim to know how to care or provide for six children any more than any other parent on the planet. I just know that we have a testimony and confirmation of having found and gathered our family. Our numbers have settled, now, as if we have finally all been accounted for, as if finding each other required enduring the same kind of bad dates as Nathan and I both had before we found each other to get married. It's been a journey for all of us, and now we can call it home.

There are days when, as a mother, I have had to put on my big bad meanie pants, like when seven-month-old Kyrie expected me to carry her around everywhere like a newborn, just because she was cute. *You know you are supposed to practice crawling, you little punk.* I had coddled her before, when they said she was sick, but whenever they said she was better, getting her to move was way more protective of her lungs than keeping her still. But that didn't stop me from feeling mixed emotions as I plopped her down two feet from her play mat where all her favorite toys were waiting.

Sometimes, I have had to put on my ill-fitting, infinite patience pants, like on a day when I was barely getting work done, and the call came to pick up my two three-year-olds from preschool. They had been suspended! It seems that the little reactive attachment disorder toddler, who never feels very safe outside the house, was not happy with getting a new teacher in her class, and tried to beat her up. Her "twin" brother started kicking and hitting, because that's what he grew up knowing, so he is always ready for a fight. I called their therapist (even though I am one), and had a family meeting with people two feet tall, and tried to be very serious about the whole thing.

When I thought it was all settled, the phone rang again, only this time about one of the first graders — a first grader who maybe locked another child in the bathroom stall for being mean to his sister. "Bad guys who are mean to girls go to jail, mom. You said so!"

And when I thought it was all settled, the phone rang again, this time about another first grader — maybe one who thought it was funny to try out a swear word during a math test, and who then maybe thought it was okay to throw a baby fit, just in case that got him out of the test entirely. It did.

And when I thought it was all settled, the phone rang again, this time about the other first grader — maybe one who took stickers from the dentist to school in effort to try and bribe other children to be her friends, because everyone was being mean to her for "talking deaf." Sigh.

And then there are days when I have to strap on my full-body, humiliation-resistant hazmat suit, like the Sunday during one of our Ohio trips when, after church, our children were congregated on the sidewalk outside. I saw a girl in a motorized wheelchair heading their way. Since our family is practically a museum of special needs, I was excited to see this meeting of children who, in some ways, must have a lot in common. When I realized she was actually just trying to get past, I was less excited to see that my children didn't think to move out of the way, forcing her to drive over onto the grass to get around them. Not only that, I was mortified to hear Kirk shout out, "Hey! Someone cut off your hands and feet! How did they get cut them off? Who cut off your hands and feet?"

I quickly corralled the little monsters into the van, and gave them a fierce Mama lecture: all of us have different hair colors, different eye colors, different skill sets, and different challenges. I reminded Kirk about how he feels when people are mean to him about his physical challenges, and asked him why he hadn't instead approached the girl with his own story, and asked her about her experiences instead of just screaming at her as she rolled passed. His reply? He said it was because he actually wanted to know how to get his own hand cut off, "because sometimes mine hurts me really bad, and her wheelchair has a motor and mine doesn't." So even what looked abrasive really wasn't once we got under the layers. Children are pretty amazing when they aren't busy botching it up, or when adults don't get in the way.

I never know what to expect when I wake up. It might be the kind of day when I have to pray to discern what is behavior and what is trauma, what is acting out and what is crying out, what is children needing to be gathered and what is children needing to be grounded. It's always a surprise.

It might be the kind of day when all their emotions come flooding out, about which parents love them and which ones don't, about who will play with them and who won't, about how scared they are for the baby, about how worried they are that the baby and I will go away again. Maybe they still don't entirely believe that we really live here and won't be homeless tomorrow, maybe they still don't entirely believe that they are really safe now, and maybe they are scared we won't have enough food — even when I take them back to look at all the food storage we have, just in case.

Or it might be like the kind of day when I went to sign home school releases for all five children, because God told me to, even though that seemed crazy as all get out. I couldn't help but notice the principal didn't really try to stop me, and maybe he reached a little too quickly to open the door for me on my way out.

Those are the kinds of days when motherhood seems more messy than shiny, and all of it hard. Those are the kind of days we have around here, but we are just as likely to be surprised by the sweet letter written in first grade cursive, or spontaneous hugs from preschoolers, or blessings called down upon our heads by tender bedtime prayers. These have made motherhood, even on the hardest days, most holy.

Nathan told me on our honeymoon that the Savior both sanctifies and justifies us. He said justification is just like what you do with the margins of a book — it spreads the text perfectly to the edges, even when it doesn't have enough characters to get there on its own. Sanctification is how the rest of those spaces get filled in. I definitely don't have enough character to smooth my margins, and need all the help I can get from the process of sanctification.

Sanctification happens through my own repentance, as I plead and cry and pray before sacrament one week, try harder the next week, and come crawling back to the altar some weeks later. Other times it happens through the sweet guidance of friends, who remind me that even hard things have purpose. Sometimes it comes through the furnace of affliction, the kind that burns to endure but helps me see more clearly. Usually, though, it happens through the children, who teach me far more than I teach them, and who so often try to trick me into releasing the inner demons I have already promised to slay.

Trying to do better is what keeps me on my knees, which keeps me closer to our Father, which is the only thing that will get us all home together... if I can try not to spill the children the way they so often spill the soup. God is more trustworthy with my soul. Instead of spilling me, he teaches me to serve others and love His children, which fills me up. He then asks me to turn my whole self over to Him, to consecrate myself, letting Him pour me out so that others can live. But, like the widow's oil, as long as I give myself completely, I never run dry.

When I lived by myself, my covenants were simple: I had few rules for when I did laundry or dishes or swept the floor. I lived by myself, and didn't make too many messes. I had the freedom to do what I wanted, whether that was traveling the world or growing food from the Earth.

When I got married, Nathan and I covenanted to care for each other. The mess doubled, and we both had to work in ways we never had before. Part of the blessings of doing the hard work to keep this covenant was our happiness. While we now had to consult with someone else before making plans, we still had a lot of flexibility and a high degree of freedom. We could spend our days writing together, and our evenings ballroom dancing. We even went on a ten-day tour of Israel with just a day's notice. Once, when Nathan was in Connecticut working on one of his musicals, I flew out and surprised him there. I not only got to see his show, but afterward, we kissed barefoot on the beach in the rain.

When we signed up with DHS to be foster parents, that contract was also a covenant. We made agreements for keeping our house clean, for keeping laundry done, for keeping up with the dishes. Workers showed up at our house when it was convenient for them, and our schedule was invaded by child appointments and school buses and lessons. We were required to attend court hearings, to buy new clothes for children we had never met, and spend our leisure time playing with little ones we might never see again.

It was not the easy life we had before, but it was what we had agreed to abide by. It wasn't about us, though; it was about the children. Because we kept our part of the deal, DHS also did their part in ringing the doorbell with children on the front step. A simple contract changed our lives forever. Nothing has ever been so hard as that fostering contract, but nothing has ever blessed our lives so much.

A covenant is a contract. Heavenly Father sets the terms of the contract, and we agree to abide by them. If we keep our end of the deal, He is bound to keep His also, and we receive more blessings than we even recognize. If we do not keep our end of the deal, He is no longer bound to bless us in those ways. He loves us still, and waits for us, and has already provided the atonement as promised, but we are missing out on so much more that He has to offer – the fullness of the gospel, as it is called.

When we got foster children, they would come from lives of chaos. Sometimes their pain was so heavy their smiles were gone. Sometimes they still had their smiles, because they didn't yet realize how injured they had been. Sometimes their smiles meant they no longer cared about injury — to themselves or to those around them.

But when they got here, their lives changed. This was a safe place, we would tell them. The rules of our house were there to keep it that way. It might have felt oppressive to some of them, or even harsh, but we knew this was what they needed, even before they understood why. We knew they needed regular meals, which also meant they needed to brush their teeth. They needed to get up for school, and go to school, and participate in school, which meant they also needed to go to bed on time. They needed clothes that were warm enough for winter, even if they had never worn coats and felt smothered by them. They needed socks and tennis shoes to be safe on the playground and in the school, even if they had only ever worn flip-flops.

But there is also safety in obedience. A twenty-one-month-old girl who had lived with us for over a year began having overnight visits with her mother, an exciting step right on the verge of reunification. Next came a planned weekend visit — but her mother was unable to keep her covenant of providing a safe home. The child was returned to us later that day, having survived a car wreck, and after being left with an unknown caregiver. We took her straight to the bathtub, throwing away her clothes and scrubbing the meth off her skin. They said where they found her was filthy, and that she had been wearing no clothes or diaper, and had soiled herself all over the floor. They said she had clearly gotten hungry, and had tried to feed herself by finding what looked like cereal (it wasn't), pouring it into a vase, and dumping out a whole gallon of milk on the floor. I held her and rocked her until she was calm, but her pupils were dilated and she was still shaking her head in circles and spinning her arms in the air as she came down from whatever she had breathed that morning. Obedience brings safety and happiness and freedom; disobedience brings an illusion of freedom, but ultimately, separation and broken hearts.

Our family has — all of us have — had to work very hard on not screaming and not hitting and not being mean. We have come a long way, and we absolutely have a testimony of the atonement, and forgiveness, and increased capacity to love, and the way relationships are strengthened through service. But it doesn't mean it isn't a battle every day, just to learn to be kind and gentle and careful with each other, because that is our covenant.

Another covenant requiring obedience is fasting. As part of my conversion, I had to learn how to fast authentically, that it was about more than just not eating, and that skipping a meal because I was busy didn't count. It is a conscious and intentional effort of forgoing physical nourishment to better tune in to spiritual things. I have fasted to practice becoming obedient, to beg for help with parenting, and to call down the power to do it well. I have fasted for insight and discernment, and I have fasted for both repentance and for revelation.

During a blessing I received at my chaplain training in Salt Lake City, I was told that fasting as a community would save Kyrie's life. Nathan and I tucked this away, and wondered what that would mean for her. When it was time for palate repair several months later, we talked with our bishop and asked if the ward could fast on Kyrie's behalf. Word spread quickly. Our ward fasted, other wards fasted, people of other faiths fasted. We all fasted and prayed together, for one little girl to breathe. She pulled through, that baby, and she did breathe. With her airway endangered by the release of her tongue and the closing of her palate, it was impossible for her to recover easily — yet she did. We all knew it was a miracle, and felt the confirmation of the Spirit shining so brightly through her.

Not only that, she started to get stronger. She was becoming more active. She stopped choking on her milk and started eating soft foods without aspirating. She stopped snoring at night and started making new babbling sounds all day. Her color changes happened less often, and she recovered more quickly. She could stay off oxygen long enough for a bath without turning blue, and still crawl and walk and laugh afterward. It was a slow and subtle change, something we noticed but didn't want to mention it in case we imagined it.

We didn't know until the follow-up trip to Cincinnati six weeks later that, since that community fast, her airway had finally started to grow. Her trachea wasn't collapsing. Her larynx was strong. The funky shaped epiglottis they wanted to shave was actually the size her airway should be, and just waiting for the airway to catch up. Maybe, they said, without exactly promising.

The doctors listened to her strong lungs, but noting that her chest cavity was still too small, told us she needed to run and play and laugh and sing and talk to grow more air sacks. Her tongue base was still too large, but she could mostly position herself and was doing great in speech therapy. Her palate repair was a beautiful feat, and holding strong despite it being so tight. Her airway was still too small, and the wrong shape, but her voice box was opening and closing correctly. Her doctors had so carefully watched her, and so aggressively helped her, and so cautiously waited for her to grow. She was getting stronger as she grew, and healthier as she breathed.

Every person who fasted had given her breath. I learned covenant-keeping from those who were so willing to go hungry so that a baby could breathe. It left me in awe, and even now gives me hope as she grows.

Our family will breathe through silly rolling laughing fits at the breakfast table, and we will breathe through mid-morning tantrums. We will breathe through songs and scripture study, and we will breathe through stories at bedtime. We will breathe at the park, and playing doll house, and playing *Star Wars*, and folding laundry. Through this life we have created together as a family, knowing to be prepared for what is yet to come, we will breathe.

# 15

Flying home with a too-small infant that isn't yours, and who is using oxygen and a feeding tube, turns out to be even more difficult than you might expect. Because we did not have a week's notice that she was released to go home, we were unable to get an Angel Flight and were expected to come up with the cash to pay for our trip. Because she was sometimes using oxygen, and needed the suctioning machine on hand, we had to fill out special papers to make arrangements with the airline. Because she had the feeding tube and its extra equipment, we had to time flights carefully so that I would be able to feed her safely. Because she was a foster child, I had to keep her placement papers and caseworker contact information easily accessible in her giant bag of medical supplies.

Standing in line at the airport made our trip home feel more real, with some anxiety that it might only be another dream from which I might be awakened by monitor alarms or a resident ready for rounds. When it was our turn to go through security, I heaved all of Kyrie's equipment up onto the conveyor belt a piece at a time, then her travel bag with food and supplies, and then unstrapped her from the carrier I wore on my chest. I got pulled aside for both of us to be checked by hand (an experience I am too familiar with because of my cochlear implants) and grew weary waiting as they proceeded to check her formula bottles one by one because they had dry powders in them, which I insisted was formula and thickener.

When we finally were cleared to proceed, I slipped Kyrie back into the carrier and strapped it back onto my chest without any help, and wondered at the skills I had learned since leaving home. I loaded my back and shoulders with her equipment, once again wishing the Life Flight to Cincinnati had let us bring her stroller. My back ached and my shoulders burned by the time I found our gate, and I was relieved to set down her things.

When it was twenty minutes until time to board, I laid Kyrie on my lap to get her as comfortable as I could, and pulled out her bag of feeding supplies. Careful that none of her tubes or syringes touched anything around me, I prepared her formula and connected the syringe to the tube still taped to her face. I flushed the tube with water to be sure it was ready, and then ignored the stares from people nearby as I lifted the open syringe into the air to pour in her formula. I tickled her chin as her tummy began to fill.

When she was finished, I flushed the tube with water again, and then gave her two different syringes of medicine. Giving the tube a final flush, I clipped the cap closed and re-taped it to her back. I dropped all the supplies into a plastic bag, and shoved that into my backpack. Happy to have eaten, Kyrie gurgled at me as people continued to stare — first because of the unusual sight of the feeding tube, and then because she charmed them with her unstoppable cuteness.

With one last diaper change, we were ready to board. They let us on early, knowing it would take time to get all her equipment settled. I was grateful when they even moved my neighbor to a better spot, leaving the seat next to me open to care for her as we traveled home. Sleepy but too curious and smart to miss out on stimulation from a brand new environment, Kyrie sat on my lap, bright and alert as other passengers filed in. After people found their seats, the stewardess gave the usual safety demonstration. As she finished the offer for mixed beverages, she pointed to Kyrie and announced into the microphone, "We are also taking requests for autographs by the little girl from *Monsters, Inc.*, riding with us today in the third row." Everyone laughed and clapped for her, delighting her to no end as she joined them in laughing and trying to clap.

Often when I work in the temple, it seems that my body can go all day with no rest and little food and almost not notice. But when the day of service is finished, and I step from that celestial turf back into the real world, my body is exhausted and famished by the time I reach my car. That's how I felt flying home with Kyrie. I had endured separation from Nathan, for which our early days of marriage had prepared me, but which was far more difficult than we knew at the time. I had gotten only very little and sporadic sleep as I fed and suctioned Kyrie all day and all night for so many weeks. I worked hard to stay afloat in deep waters, buoyed up from prayers from so far away, but my skin hungered for that of my husband. I had heard disaster stories and celebrated their successes with my children through video phone calls, but ached to hug them and run my fingers through their hair.

When we landed at Tulsa International Airport, I wasn't sure I could even make it to the concourse where everyone would be waiting. My eyes were running over with fatigue and relief, for sure, as I walked through the last doors that separated me from the most precious people in my life.

*There they are!*

My husband! My children! And so many wonderful friends. The children ran to me so fast that they set off the alarms at the security gate. I dropped everything but the baby, collapsed into Nathan, and cried like a girl, feeling all my children surround me. I was so very glad to be home. *Home.*

Everyone had grown so much! Anber was a toddler when I left, a defiant two-year-old with a baby face. Now she was three! She had grown almost five inches, no joke, and looked like a little girl instead of a baby. I couldn't believe how big she was!

Alex was suddenly playing a big brother role that I had always wanted to him to have, but wasn't sure if it would ever click. But he had figured it out! Sometimes it was still hard, as he learned the difference between leadership and domination, but his sisters were always quick to remind him that he definitely wasn't the boss of them. He had become so very helpful and cooperative, and my little gentleman. He was still Alex, though, and still got into the craziest antics, and could make me laugh like nothing else.

Kind and gentle, Kirk was usually our "good kid", but got into some trouble while I was gone. It was the kind of trouble that revealed to us a piece of his past, and it wasn't until I got home that the story spilled out in words instead of behaviors. Once he got it off his chest, he felt much better, and was back to just being Kirk. I was so relieved!

Barrett had come so far! He was still throwing spoiled tantrums, a behavior that had been thoroughly ingrained in him by a previous foster family, but at least now he was starting to regulate and calm down when prompted. He was more easily entreated, more easily redirected, and generally happier than I had ever seen him. This was also a huge relief to me, because with some children, it's hard to see progress while you are in the trenches. That new, ear-to-ear smile of his could light up a room! It reminded me of Mary, who never smiled when she first came to us the year before, but now had the heartiest laugh ever.

My return home also came with big news for Mary. We had found out that same day that we were one step closer to becoming her adoptive parents. Both biological parents had agreed to relinquish rights, and the hearing to do so was finally set for fall. Since she had already lived with us beyond the required six-month minimum waiting period, her adoption date could be set as soon as termination was completed. She was so excited! She and Anber especially loved being sisters, and had created a pretty special bond while I was gone.

We stopped to eat on the way back to normalcy, having a sit-down celebration where the children even got to drink soda, which made it a red letter day. As we regrouped after the airport excitement, the children began sharing their experiences from while I had been away. They said, "We're glad you are back, because Daddy finally decided he was the boss around here." I laughed so hard!

Nathan really did do an amazing job! When I got home, the house was clean, and the children had been well cared for the whole time. He got Mary's long, kinky hair washed, and with help from a caseworker got it rebraided again until I got home. He even cut their nails! I was so impressed!

He had been worried about the children not doing as much schoolwork every day as when I am the taskmaster, but he kept it simple and consistent, so they did not lose any skills over the summer and continued to make progress. School would be starting soon, and it seemed like they were ready.

Nathan and I both agreed, in hindsight, that we could see the wisdom Heavenly Father had in assigning me to do chaplaincy training all that spring, pulling me out of the home for a night at a time, and then a weekend at a time, so that Nathan got to gain skills and confidence before suddenly being left with six children by himself for six weeks. He did so great, I can't tell you!

Coming home now, I could feel that something had shifted with us as a family, something that was better balanced, and more as it should be, but in a way it could not have happened before. So much was changing, that now this was really-really our family! This was it! We were set! I was a mom, finally, miraculously.

And our miracle girl? She was a miracle, alright. After we were back and settled, Kyrie went in for re-assessments with the early intervention team, and she aced everything. Her pediatrician was also pleased with her progress, and no one could believe how well she was doing. When we finished all those appointments, I went straight to DHS to catch up on all the children's cases, and everyone was so glad to see her and that she was doing so well.

Those appointments were our last big outing for a while, because we needed to enter an isolation period. Having been in such a tightly controlled environment for so long, Kyrie's immune system needed some time to re-adjust to her new family and our germs, before we all got back to our lives. The children, with their attachment issues, also needed some serious bonding time with no distractions. And besides that, I almost didn't want to let any of them out of my sight ever again.

Looking back, I see this as a kind of Golden Age of Kyrie's early childhood. Her body responded so vigorously to finally being able to breathe that she had a growth spurt, and within two months had almost outgrown the gains she had suffered through distraction to win. Soon, she would be back on oxygen as she outgrew her brand new airway, initiating her cycle of periodic pneumonia and severe desats. Nathan and I would also begin our cycle of frustration with medical specialists unable to discern any problems that would be causing it.

But for that short honeymoon, Kyrie was eating, breathing, and thriving! At five months old, she outgrew her newborn clothes almost overnight, gaining a whole pound just in the first week after leaving Cincinnati. It was the first time ever that she had gained weight at home. Her feet doubled in size, no joke, so she even got to wear real shoes instead of just baby socks. This was our life, our very real and amazing life!

Keeping Kyrie alive that first year took a lot of time, energy, money, emotion, support, and supplies. The judge over her case ordered me to present an accounting of all of it. I was supposed to prepare a detailed report on each of these aspects of her care for a staffing at court — a meeting that prepared the DA for moving to petition for termination of parental rights. I had been to staffings before for consults as a counselor, but with all of the children who had come through our home, this was a first as a foster parent. I was anxious, and seemed to feel a lot hanging on the success of my presentation.

I was told I would be asked about Kyrie's ongoing medical issues, the severity of them and the danger when she was in crisis, how normal she looked when she was doing well, how quickly that could change at any moment, and how hard she was fighting. After discussing this request with Nathan, I thought about how I would describe this to the judge. I decided to share what it was like to lay Kyrie down at night, not knowing if she would wake in the morning; what it was like to hold her screaming in pain because no pain medicine worked in her drug baby body; what it was like to hold vigil for her on life support, to whack her in the chest when her heart stops, and to shake her awake from being purple and cold.

There was plenty of equipment she needed, of course. There were suctioning machines so that she didn't drown in her own saliva, oxygen tanks, a concentrator that made oxygen from room air for her, a travel concentrator for the car and appointments, monitors for her heart and for her apnea and for her oxygen levels, all the tubing and stickers that oxygen requires, all the supplies for NG tubes, and a dozen different kinds of tapes for alternating so that her newborn skin isn't eaten by all the adhesives. All of this required training in order to be used safely.

They also asked me to bring the budget and receipts of all that Medicaid didn't cover, and that we had personally spent on her trying to keep her alive, in part so that they could review with the biological parents what they would need to be able to provide for her. They also requested a list of each and every appointment she had had, noting which two out of hundreds were the only appointments the parents had attended in nine months.

I was told the judge, the judge's case manager, all the attorneys, the caseworker and supervisor, Kyrie's attorney, and the DA would be present. It was important for the parents to attend as well, but they did not show up. They had not even contacted us to ask how the baby was doing, though I had sent them pictures of her distractors, her sleep study wires, her on the airplane home, the picture of all of us at the temple, and her adorable dog-earred ponytails. It was at that meeting that I first heard about "immediate termination", which was later explained to me as meaning the case was so "heinous and shocking" that termination could happen right away and without a trial.

The biological parents were notified that the DA was filing a motion to terminate their parental rights. A court date was issued, and they signed the notice that informed them of when it was. The caseworker reminded them, and I reminded them. I even told them I had new pictures of her repaired palate to show them, as well as artwork from Anber for the mother.

The day came. The hour arrived. The parents did not.

While the court waited, the evidence was explained, and the caseworker updated the judge. Still no biological parents.

Then the judge said something I couldn't understand, banged her gavel, and winked at me. "She's a beautiful baby," I heard her add.

I smiled and nodded. *What just happened?* I missed it.

The lady carrying files nodded me toward the door, letting me know our case was finished for the day. I stood up and walked out, waiting for Kyrie's caseworker to come out of the court room. When she did, she was pale as anything, and excitedly whispered, "I can't believe that just happened!"

Confused, I asked for clarification, telling her I had missed hearing when the next court date was. I pulled my phone to put it in my schedule right away. The caseworker pulled my phone down so she could look me straight in the eye.

"You got her! She's your baby!"

"What?!"

"The judge just terminated. It's done. The next court date will be her adoption. She's yours!"

I busted out an ugly cry right there on the stairs, until one of the bailiffs had to move me out of the way. I hugged the caseworker and her supervisor, and cried all the way to the car. I couldn't believe it. *How, after everything, could it be so simple?* Even in that moment, my heart fluttered a bit at the thought of her mother. *Where were you? How could you just not show up?* I assumed it meant she was using again, but this relapse had cost her a second daughter. There was more paperwork and another court date to actually finalize the adoption, but that's how she became ours. *We were keeping Kyrie!*

Kyrie's graduation into adoptive placement also marked a shift in our transition out of fostering. I still didn't want fostering just to be taken away from me. I had experienced too many sudden losses beyond my control, and I wanted to let it go consciously, with closure, in good and healthy ways. But now we had six children at home. Ours. For keeps. Our focus had to move from "serving children" to "building a home".

I was yearning for the temple, where having children sealed to our family for eternity would be such a different experience than the previous flailing about without an anchor. No matter how much we loved those children who passed through our lives, it's hard to fully bond and fully attach when you don't know how long they will be there and when they don't know if they get to stay. It's so complicated. And our family was hungry for stability and permanency.

When we had been notified that Alex and Anber's cases were both being sent to jury trial, we were anxious. We had no idea what would happen, no way to prepare them, and no guarantees that it would result in termination. It all felt so much like our pregnancies had been: we knew there was a child, but didn't know if that meant the beginning of our family, or only a precious few months of mortality shared together before saying goodbye. We wanted them to be able to stay, but also grieved with them the loss of their parents — a feeling I knew only too well.

Alex and Anber both became legally free for adoption within weeks of each other, and the timing was perfect. They had come to us so close together, and had lived with us for so long, that they already felt like they belonged together. Their cases were entirely unrelated, so it would have to be two separate adoptions, but the court was happy to coordinate so that we could do both on the same day.

Finalizing our first adoptions was crazy exciting, even at a time that was already full of anticipation. Kyrie had not been born yet, but was due within weeks. Kirk and Barrett weren't living with us yet, but we had already started our play dates.

Mary struggled as all the adoption attention focused on Alex and Anber. We were waiting to find out whether or not she would stay with us to be adopted or be moved to live with extended family. Meanwhile, we found out that the DA was filing to terminate rights on her mother around the same time. That was a lot for her to process. She kept getting excited about the possibility of adoption, but struggled to understand that it would mean not seeing her mother anymore, except on scheduled visits we approved when she was clean and out of jail.

So, we made sure that, just like Alex and Anber got new and fancy clothes for adoption day, Mary also got to pick out new clothes. We even let her wear her new fancy Easter shoes, and we asked Nathan's parents to pick her up from school early enough to go out to lunch before court. There is nothing like grandparents to help you feel special and loved.

The children were too excited to go to bed easily the night before, and woke as early as if it were Christmas. That morning was rainy, but with sunshine, and the children ran through the house screaming, "Sun shower! Sun shower!" while I was trying to get them dressed.

We had an hour's drive to court because no one told us yet that we could do the adoptions in the county where we lived. The ride was lovely, until we got half-way there, and Anber suddenly threw up her entire breakfast. I scrounged around in the van, finding an old pajama shirt and a pull-up for her to wear. We cleaned her up with the help of a stranger, who had pulled over to offer us some paper towels. In the next town on our way, we stopped to pick up some tummy medicine, and to buy Anber a new dress for court.

We pulled in to a gas station for a bathroom break and to get Anber dressed. Two things happened there. First, Anber saw some lady she said was Grandma Neen (my mom, Jeanine), and ran to her like I have never seen her run to anyone. She hugged her up, and talked to her for a long time. This was unheard of, as Anber never talked at all outside the home. The lady was very nice, and really did look a little like my mom. I have no idea who the lady was, but it was very special that Anber made my mom a part of adoption day.

The other thing that happened was Alex had a serious allergy attack, one of the worst he has ever had before or since. He had not eaten anything he was allergic to, so we could only attribute it to the spring air. At any rate, we had to rush back to the pharmacy again to get him medicine and eye drops.

It was a wild day. It felt as if extra opposition was being heaped up against us. And when we thought about adoption as the final step before taking these children to be sealed to us in the temple, that idea of the opposition against us made a lot of sense.

We were relieved to finally arrive at the courthouse, and couldn't believe we were still on time. Stepping inside, we were delighted to see that the Claremore police officers who had originally worked on Alex and Anber's cases had come to see them be adopted. Alex ran to them, and Anber ran away from them. Both cases had been featured in the local news, because both children had been picked up within weeks of each other at the casino, and so a camera crew was also there to interview us about their adoptions and the need for more foster parents. It was all very exciting, and only got the children more hyped up while we waited for their turn in court.

But they did have to wait. And wait. And wait.

Finally, our adoption attorney came out and called me and Nathan to the judge's chambers. "We have a problem," she murmured.

I gulped.

As we sat down at the heavy table too big for the small room, our adoption attorney explained that the DA forgot to file the termination order for Alex's case. The parental rights for Alex had been terminated when his mother did not show up for court and when his father lost the jury trial, so that was done. "But even with a jury trial deciding termination," she explained, "an order still has to be filed on record."

It had not been filed, and that meant Alex was not yet legally free to be adopted.

I could not hold back my tears, and Nathan held me tightly.

Worse, once the paperwork was actually filed, they would have to wait another thirty days before scheduling the adoption date due to a required appeal period for the biological parents. The waiting period could not be waived, and there was no way around it. Alex could not be adopted that day.

*How am I supposed to go out there, after all he has been through, and tell that little boy he isn't getting adopted today?*

The attorneys and judge were very apologetic, and very upset with the DA for not having finished the paperwork, but none of that was any help to Alex.

Controlling the mix of hurt, anger, frustration, and betrayal that I felt, I emphatically insisted that they had better come up with a plan because that boy was not going home without his day in court. He wasn't just a foster child who had waited more than two years for adoption; he was a foster child with autism who had rehearsed this day repeatedly — specifically because we needed him to say his new name in the courtroom, and we had to be sure he didn't name himself SpiderMan CaptainAmerica as he planned. They agreed that, after Anber's adoption was final and the court record was closed, the judge would come down to take pictures with us as a family, and that he would find a way to let Alex say his new name.

Anber's adoption was a beautiful and poignant moment, a culmination of three years of struggle, a reminder of the grief and all she had endured, and the settling of the trust with her we had tried so hard to build. We really could now promise her — and literally did in court — that she would stay with us, that we would care for her, and that we would meet her needs. She was officially named Anber, which was a fragment of the name she brought with her. We gave her one middle name from my mother, and another from Nathan's, and she was the first child to take our last name. She was not yet three that day, but she visibly relaxed as she watched this scene, and her knots have slowly loosened into smiles and laughter every day since.

When her adoption was final, the judge said in a booming voice, "Young man?" and pointed his gavel at Alex.

Our almost-but-not-yet son shot up from his seat and saluted, "Yes, sir!"

"I hear you are getting adopted next. Could you please announce your new adoption name so that I will know what to call you when you come back into my court room?"

"Yes, sir!" Alex shouted his name at the top of his lungs, one syllable at a time, giving his new middle names from my father and Nathan's, proud as anything. He then bolted out into the hallway and pulled the fire alarm. That was our first adoption day.

By the time Alex's adoption was finalized a month later, we knew that Mary was going to be staying with us, but she was still not yet legally free for adoption. The court date for termination of parental rights was scheduled months away, and we weren't sure it would actually happen even then. Kirk and Barrett were moved in with us by then, though, and it was fun for them to come and see an adoption before it was their turn. Kyrie had been born, but was still in the hospital in Oklahoma City, and we knew nothing other than that her condition was critical.

On a bright Saturday morning, we took Alex and Anber to the temple together. Alex was unusually stately in his white, three-piece suit that would later be passed down to Kirk. Anber's dress was so big on her that day that it dragged on the ground, but would be mid-calf length by the time Kyrie was sealed to us. My brother's teenagers stayed with Kirk and Barrett and Mary in the foyer of the temple, while Alex and Anber came back to join us in a sealing room overflowing with loved ones. That sacred priesthood sealing ordinance was just one moment in mortality, but will hold us together for eternity.

When we had finished at the temple, and changed back into less conspicuous street clothes, we drove downtown to Children's Hospital to visit Kyrie. Because her condition was so fragile, Anber, as the biological half-sister, was the only sibling allowed to visit her. Nathan sat with the others as I took Anber with me to see her new sister for the first time. She stood on a rocking chair, peeking over the side of the plastic bassinet, the way Alex had once peeked over to meet Anber for the first time. Kyrie's oxygen and feeding tubes scared Anber, but she also didn't want to leave. She whispered to her, and sang her a little song, and we worked together to tape up pictures of Anber and our whole family, so that Kyrie would not be alone while we were away.

When it was Nathan's turn to see her, he quietly closed the door, placed fingers on her sleeping head, and gave her a blessing. She would receive the care that she needed, would be surrounded by those who love her, and would live to fulfill her mission in mortality. Even though we were not yet allowed to stay, and could not yet bring her home, Father-in-Heaven knew her, and she would not be alone.

Mary assumed her adoption would be next, since she had lived with us for almost two years already, but Kirk and Barrett's six-month trial period passed before Mary's case had made it that far. Even less impressed this time, Mary stomped along with us for their adoption while complaining that it was supposed to be her turn. It was a challenging thing, to let Kirk and Barrett pick their adoption breakfast, and to discuss adoption party plans with them, and still find ways to help Mary feel special. Finally, two days before the boys got adopted, Nathan and I got to sign the papers that transitioned Mary from foster child to adoptive placement. She made sure everyone knew how she beat Kirk and Barrett to being "an adoption kid". It wasn't exactly true, but the boys didn't mind and it seemed to put her at ease.

As with the other children, it was important to us to stay in contact with the biological parents and extended family as much as was possible and safe to do so. Kirk and Barrett's biological parents — their shared mother and the two fathers — had relinquished their parental rights before we ever met the boys. But while the fathers had not had any contact, the mother was young and seemed to be trying hard. She was clean, and had a job, and was responsive when we tried to communicate with her.

We set up a private page online for Kirk and Barrett, like we had for the other children, so their biological families could get updates on them. One of the boys' grandmothers worked at the gas station around the corner from our home, so we could stop by and say hello. Another grandmother mailed them new clothes — and later, clothes for all the children.

While we could do nothing about any of the biological parents having lost custody of their children, we could do our best to make sure they didn't lose them completely. As often as we could, we held "parent parties" at the playground for post-adoption visits. Kirk and Barrett's aunt and uncle came frequently, while other relatives traveling through town sometimes surprised them as well. The boys' mother also came, and as we got to know her through these visits, we felt prompted to do a very hard thing for all of us: we invited her to their adoption.

She came, and it was a beautiful gift to her boys. Her face was red with tears the whole time, but she had a smile they could see, and she hugged them and congratulated them, and endured picture taking afterward. The love she had for her boys was palpable that day, and I can't imagine how hard it was for her to come watch them be adopted by someone else. But with courage and the drive to do what was best for them, she did it. Her presence with us that day was one of the most tangible acts of service and love that I have ever experienced in my life.

Mary waited four more months for her adoption, and it was a hard four months. Her mother went back to jail. Mary had surgery for her second cochlear implant. But hardest of all, Mary's beloved biological grandfather, with whom she had a special bond, passed away. He had been cutting grass with a riding lawn mower, and on a hill, it rolled over onto him. We visited him daily in the hospital, and then several times a week once he was sent home, but he never recovered from his injuries.

Nathan took Mary to her grandfather's funeral while I was in that staffing for Kyrie where I had to testify about all we had done to keep her alive. Mary saw her mother there, and met her mother's new boyfriend, and had a bit of a healthy confrontation to express some of the things she had been holding in for so long. Mostly, though, the visit was as good as it could be for a funeral, in the way hearts tend to soften when a loved one has passed.

The passing of Mary's grandfather also brought us a precious gift: more of Mary's extended family. She got to know an aunt and a cousin and an uncle and a few others, who were so kind to her and promised to remain in touch. We also received notes about her genealogy, which I had requested weeks before the mowing accident. Mary's grandfather had jotted down some names and dates for me, and his fiancé had found them for me on the counter after he passed.

Mary still struggles to connect "with my black family" from her father's side, specifically craving to understand more about that part of her identity. We can teach her about history, and take her to museums, and read her books. I have even learned how to braid her hair in less than four hours. But I cannot *be* something I have not lived, no matter how important it is for her to know. Some of this she and Anber will have to learn through their own experiences. It's like being Deaf: I can teach her sign language, and model culture for her, but Mary had to go to the Deaf school and immerse herself in the experience for her to connect with that part of her identity.

When Mary's adoption day finally came, she almost didn't believe us. While we were discussing what new outfit she might want to wear to court, she also realized that we would not be able to invite her mother as we had Kirk and Barrett's mother, because "my mother will just boss everyone and be crazy, and not listen or be happy." Also because her mother was back in jail again. But wanting her to still feel loved by her biological family, I pointed out that we would have invited her grandfather if he were still alive. Connecting this in her little head, and always being a princess-girl who loves a good holiday, Mary decided to wear the beautiful, red-lace dress that her grandfather had gotten her to wear at his wedding. That's what she wore to her Valentine's week adoption hearing — while also insisting that all of her now-official siblings also wear red.

They looked adorable, though it was past the season for their Christmas clothes. As soon as we stepped out of the courthouse, Mary was quick to point out that she was officially the oldest, and boss of them all. This was the heated discussion all the way to the temple, where the removal of fiery red and donning of pure white became even more symbolic in that quiet and gentle space. Something healed in Mary that day when she was sealed to us with all her siblings (except Kyrie) watching, something that gave her peace and made her smile. It was a day all her own, exactly as she needed it to be.

Waiting there, in the celestial room before Mary's sealing, Nathan and I couldn't help but think back on how hard we had prayed for children. Maybe we prayed a little too hard. Nathan said that it was a little bit like that Old Testament story where the Israelites in the wilderness are complaining about having manna every day, and the Lord says, "You want quail? I'll give ya quail till it comes out your ears!"

Beginning with Alex and Anber, and then finding Mary, and then choosing Kirk and Barrett, and then finally bringing Kyrie home made us a family. Besides a house full of so many little ones, we had hit the official number limit for fostering. We were willing to occasionally still help with emergencies or respite care, but DHS could no longer place with us.

We were done fostering, officially, completely. No more drug babies, no more overnight kiddos, no more last minute placements just until they could find an available foster home. We were finished, our house was full, and our family was whole. We had given all we could give. I had my closure, and I felt that mantle lift from me as I let it go.

We knew we would still have years of parenting ahead of us, obviously, and that adoption and sealing were a beginning as much as an ending. There would be other battles, and other hard days, even after our children were grown. But this piece: the gathering of our children through fostering, and the making every moment count, and the swimming in devotion to these children even when I have no idea how to help them — that we have done well. Not perfectly, not without mistakes, and not without already having at least one encounter with the police. But, in one of the few areas of my life, for maybe the first time in my life, I can honestly say that I have done my very absolute best and given all I had to give.

And I hadn't missed a moment. I gave up working at LDS Family Services, because I needed to be home with the children. I gave up extra income from hospital shifts, because I needed to be home with the children. I gave up a comfortable living, because I needed to be home with the children – who are so very expensive, by the way, even without any frills. I gave up the time I used to spend in study, and I gave up the time I used to play with friends, and I gave up the organization of my home. But I got these babies, all six children, who are beautiful and wonderful and hilarious... and *home*.

What better time to start clearing out junk? Nathan and I picked a Saturday to start our assault on the garage. We no longer needed clothes for any possible child of any possible age in any possible season. We passed them along.

I tossed the bassinet to Nathan from across the garage, and threw the newborn swing at him, and flew the play mat like a Frisbee. We pulled out Barrett's car seat from the van, because he finally got to move into a booster. We booted Barrett and Anber's booster chairs from the dinner table. We downsized a stroller, and passed it along.

When we started fostering, or even before that, when my mother died, I had thought this day would come too soon and be too hard. In the middle of those years of grief, when I lost both my parents and my babies, I expected letting go of physical memories would wrench my gut beyond what I could handle. It would be what finally knocked me over a very precarious cliff, I thought.

That bassinet? It's not just a girly baby bed with ruffles and pink. It's where we laid her on her side and elevated, because she couldn't breathe on her back. It's where we glued monitors to her every night, so that we would wake every time she stopped breathing. It's where we rushed when the alarms warned us her heart had stopped again.

The little newborn rocker? It's not just a cute swing in all its pink glory. It's where we rocked her on her side after feeding her through a tube, trying to keep it all from coming back up.

The motorized swing? It wasn't just a gift from a friend, but a symbol of love. That friend twice drove the baby all the way to me at the hospital in Tulsa where I was working, just because of feeding crises and to help get her back to sleep. That friend rocked her and fed her and loved her, when others were too afraid to try to help.

The first walker, the one she already wore out? A miracle. Because she wasn't supposed to live this long. And here she was, outgrowing clothes and toys faster than I would like. But that is good and right, and as it should be.

And the baby clothes? Any mother will tell you how hard it is to let go of tiny clothes. Kyrie wore her preemie clothes for six months, and her newborn clothes for another four months. It wasn't about the cuteness of those little outfits; it was about the smell of memories that wafted through the air when I touched them, and how days that were once so overwhelming have now passed by so quickly.

This was the first outfit I took to her in the hospital, where she had been wearing only a diaper and a thousand tubes and cords for fifty-one days. This was the outfit I brought her home in, when we drove straight to the temple across town for me to pray my Hannah-tears over this little Samuel-baby-girl who was a miracle, my miracle. This was the outfit she was wearing when Nathan held her for the first time, when she smiled for the first time, when we gave her the specialty bottle she finally took instead of only the feeding tube. These are the pants that matched that adorable shirt we had to cut off when we resuscitated her. This is the dress she was wearing that time we rode in the ambulance, the shorts she was wearing when we were Life-Flighted, the sleeper she was wearing when we took her last pictures before surgery when she didn't wake up and lay there on life support. This is what she was wearing when we finally came home again, on the airplane, or when we flew on another airplane out to Utah, or when we called the ambulance again and they were sure we had lost her. This is what she was wearing when I knew, *I knew*, she was our baby and staying in our family.

I had thought letting go would be unbearable. But it was perfect, exactly perfect. I wasn't cheated out of anything. It didn't happen until I was ready. And then it was right. It was right, and a relief.

It's not about the clothes, anyway. It's about the sacred and precious memories, and the love that grows through those experiences. When Kyrie was a year old, she finally moved into the hand-me-down clothes we had saved from Anber, as if it was always meant to be.

When Kyrie was finally legally free, her adoption caseworker and attorney worked especially hard to rush things. Kyrie was not doing well. We were on the verge of her third trip to Cincinnati, and everyone felt an urgency about finalizing her adoption. We wanted to be sure to have consent for health care decisions, and we knew we had a divine promise that she would be sealed to us before she died — which we hoped was still a long way off.

Once again, though, the termination order had not been filed on time. Kyrie's adoption date was still within the grace period for parental appeal — by one day. This time the DA had actually filed the order, just not right away. Understanding the urgency of the situation, the judge called for a special session of family court, just for us. We were relieved we would still have consent rights before she was hospitalized again, but this also meant that we would have to leave straight from the courthouse to the temple for Kyrie's sealing, and then start out that night for Ohio in order to arrive in time for another week of scopes, sleep and swallow studies, and surgeries.

Kyrie was just barely a year old when her adoption was finalized. Instead of charming the judge from the over-sized attorney chairs at the front table, as the other children had done, Kyrie stood on the table itself, dancing and waving to everyone in the courtroom, while trying to lasso Nathan with her oxygen cord. She smiled and waved when they said her new name, and giggled when the judge banged the gavel that made her ours.

We left the courthouse quickly, not stopping for a celebratory meal this time. Our goal was, and had been for a year, to get that baby to the temple while she was still breathing. The children changed from their fancy court clothes into their white temple clothes, with the ever-growing Alex in his third white suit since his own sealing. None of their shoes fit anymore. Tiny Kyrie, on the other hand, still had not grown into her dress, which swallowed her in ruffles, even though I had made sure to only get a size six-month dress and she was over a year old.

For the first time, and for the last time until they are grown someday, we were able to take all six of our children into the temple with us that afternoon. Alex and Anber had gone first, and then returned with us for Kirk and Barrett's turn. When Mary was sealed to us, everyone but Kyrie got to go back with us. For Kyrie, we were finally all there together in the sealing room — plus fifty feet of oxygen tubing and the travel concentrator. *What does this mean for them, that they got to come back to the sealing room so many times, to hear and see the things they have witnessed at their young ages?*

In temples all over the world, in the rooms where sealings are performed by the authority and power of the priesthood, there hang two large mirrors on opposite walls, giving a hint at eternity in their reflections. I gazed at the faces of my husband and my extraordinary children, all dressed in white and tangled in a group hug that probably wasn't quite temple-reverent, and saw happiness reflected and multiplied in a multiplicity of blessings. There, in the mirrors, filling my vision, were the generations before us and the generations yet to come. I knew that we had witnessed the formation of our family, the creation of order from the chaos, the miracle of what it meant to be alive — to find and become a forever family.

*Emily with her mother, Jeanine, shortly before Emily married Nathan in 2012.*

*Emily with Nathan on the beach after she surprised him in Connecticut in 2013.*

*Emily and Kyrie (with distractors and NG tube visible) at Cincinnati Children's Hospital in 2015.*

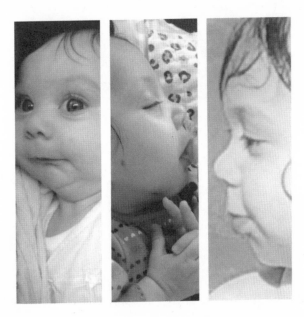

*Kyrie's chin before and immediately after distraction (left and center), and almost a year later (right).*

*All of the Christensen children together in 2016.*

*After Kyrie's sealing at the LDS temple in Oklahoma City in 2016.*

As of July 2016, Kyrie is a bright and busy toddler who continues to live life as fully as she can, and who continues to be happy in spite of all she has endured. The battle to support her airway is ongoing as she continues to grow.